Group Work with
Adolescents After
Violent Death

Group Work with Adolescents After Violent Death

A Manual for Practitioners

Alison Salloum, LCSW

Brunner-Routledge
Taylor & Francis Group

NEW YORK AND HOVE

Cover design by Patty Lipkin of Mad Dash Designs

Published in 2004 by
Brunner-Routledge
29 West 35th Street
New York, NY 10001
www.brunner-routledge.com

Published in Great Britain by
Brunner-Routledge
27 Church Road
Hove, East Sussex
BN3 2FA
www.brunner-routledge.co.uk

Copyright © 2004 by Taylor & Francis Books, Inc.
Brunner-Routledge is an imprint of the Taylor & Francis Group.

Printed in the United States of America on acid-free paper.
Typesetting: BookType

10 9 8 7 6 5 4 3 2 1

Library of Congress Cataloging-in-Publication Data

Salloum, Alison, 1966-
   Group work with adolescents after violent death : a manual for practitioners / Alison Salloum.
       p.   cm.
   Includes bibliographical references and index.
   ISBN 0-415-94861-4 (alk. paper)
   1. Group psychotherapy for teenagers—Handbooks, manuals, etc. 2. Teenagers—Counseling of—Handbooks, manuals, etc. 3. Post-traumatic stress disorder in children—Handbooks, manuals, etc. 4. Violent deaths—Psychological aspects. I. Title.

   RJ505.G7S34 2004
   616.85'210651—dc22

                                                              2004001187

Contents

Part I Understanding Adolescents After Violent Death

List of Activity Handouts

Permission is granted to photocopy these for group use.

Acknowledgments

My deepest appreciation is to Peg Reese for her support and for reading several versions of this manual. Also, I am extremely grateful for the work of Patty Lipkin with Mad Dash Designs who provided the graphics and layout for the handouts and activity worksheets.

I would also like to thank the following people: Ron McClain, LCSW, Executive Director, Children's Bureau of New Orleans, and all of the staff, especially the Project LAST team, for their support and commitment to help children and families; Michael Cunningham, PhD, Tulane University, Psychology Department, for being an excellent teacher and for reviewing sections of this manual; Judy Lewis, PhD, Tulane University, School of Social Work, for our weekly meetings that helped keep me grounded; Lou Irwin, LCSW, BCD, for contributing the meditation for adolescents; and Edward K. Rynearson, MD, for his support.

Introduction

Because of the prevalence of violence and violent death, there has been a tremendous amount of attention placed on psychological first aid or crisis intervention. Organizations, certification programs, task forces, school crisis response teams, and national crisis networks are all trained to respond to survivors and victims of mass violence, death, and/or traumatic events (see Appendix A). When the national media covers violent death, crisis responders are often close by or soon to arrive. When the crisis response workers and media have left, however, survivors and witnesses are often left alone to cope with the long-lasting effects of violence and death. For those who need support, we must let them know that help is available. For populations such as adolescents who may not seek services, outreach, and education, adolescent-specific interventions and the presence of caring adults who can assist them is crucial.

This manual provides information about ways to help adolescents who have had someone close die due to violence and/or who have witnessed violent death. Part 1 provides information about the reactions and experiences of adolescents after violent death. The main focus of the manual is group work with adolescents; however chapters 1, 3, 4, and 6 to 10 provide information that can be used by practitioners who are providing individual or family therapy with adolescents, and by teachers, probation officers, youth ministers, or any type of staff who work with adolescents after violent death. Information about adolescent bereavement, posttraumatic stress, traumatic grief, witnessing and surviving violent death, and contextual influences is presented.

Part 2 provides a step-by-step outline for providing an educational group session for parents, teachers, and staff who are in contact with adolescents who have had someone close die due to violence and/or who have witnessed violent death. These educational groups provide information about adolescent reactions after violent death, warning signs, and ways to help. It is hoped that by providing information to adults, youth in need of assistance can be identified and help can be provided.

Part 3 provides group facilitators with critical information for organizing a time-limited grief and trauma group for adolescents after violent death. Chapter 13 includes guidelines for facilitators and a post-session review handout that can be used to assist facilitators with conducting a group. Chapter 14 outlines important steps for implementing a time-limited grief and trauma group such as outreach, screening, organization, and evaluation. Chapter 15 provides facilitators with practical information for managing the group.

Part 4 describes a 10-week grief and trauma group that is designed specifically for adolescents who have had someone close die due to violence and/or who have witnessed violent death. This

xii   GROUP WORK WITH ADOLESCENTS AFTER VIOLENT DEATH

group model can be offered after a crisis intervention where all the adolescents experienced the same violent incident, or with adolescents who all have had someone close to them die due to violence at different times in their lives and/or who have witnessed violent death. Whether the violent death occurred last month or 2 years ago, the group is intended for adolescents who continue to struggle with the aftermath. Chapter 16 includes an outline of each session and handouts that can be used by the group participants.

This 10-week adolescent grief and trauma group model was designed by incorporating research and theory, which is discussed in Part 1, and practice experience. Traditional bereavement groups that do not consider the effects of violent death may not meet the unique needs of adolescents after violent death. Therefore, this model is designed to address the specific concerns of adolescents after violent deaths (accidents, suicides, and homicides), to decrease the traumatic responses that may be occurring, and to facilitate the bereavement process.

Facilitators who work with adolescents after violent death are encouraged to continue to learn more about bereavement, trauma, and the effects of violence. When offering mental health intervention after violent death, knowledge must accompany compassion. It is hoped that this manual provides theoretically sound and practical information that will be used in a compassionate manner to assist adolescents after violent death, including those youth who may not have otherwise received help.

Part I

Understanding Adolescents After Violent Death

Violent Death
(Accidents, Suicides, and Homicides)

Accidents, homicides, and suicides are the top three causes of death among 10- to 20-year-olds in the United States. Every day, an estimated 54 young people die from accidents, 16 from homicides, and 13 from suicide (Centers for Disease Control and Prevention, 2003). Given the high incidence of violent death among young people, it is not surprising that many adolescents have had friends die. In fact, in a survey of high school students, 87% indicated that they had experienced the death of a friend, and 20% indicated they have had more than one friend die. Only 13% reported that they had not experienced the death of a friend (Schachter, 1991). In another study with college students (age 17 to 20), who were from 58 high schools, 70.6% reported that they experienced the death of someone close during their high school years, with 43.5% of the deaths being the death of a peer. All of the peer deaths, except one, were the result of violence (accident, suicide, or homicide) (Ringler & Hayden, 2000).

Many adolescents have not only had friends die but also parents, siblings, aunts, uncles, teachers, neighbors, coaches, religious leaders, and other significant people. Having someone close die causes distress for most people, but when the death is caused by violence an extra layer of shock, anger, numbness, and disorientation, along with questions of "why," are often added to the grief. Having someone close, die due to violence and/or witnessing violent death can be a traumatic experience. Unfortunately, incidents in which adolescents experience traumatic events, such as witnessing violence, hearing about the death of someone close, and having a loved one die, are far from rare in the United States. For example, in a study with 1,420 children and adolescents (age 9 to 16) from a general population, one in four reported that during their lifetime they had experienced an extreme stressor. The three most common stressors were witnessing a traumatic event, learning about a traumatic event, and experiencing the death of a loved one (Costello, Erkanli, Faribank, & Angold, 2002).

Many violent deaths are preventable. Given the amount of pain and devastation adolescent survivors face, the imperative to support prevention programs becomes paramount. However, given the prevalence of violent death in the United States, prevention and intervention must occur simultaneously. Multiple strategies and approaches are needed that include policies, research, prevention and intervention programs, and national and local involvement. The Annie E. Casey Foundation has outlined an excellent multifaceted strategy to reduce teen mortality by addressing some of the underlying causes of adolescent death. This plan is not only focused on addressing risk factors such as substance abuse, gun access, seat belt enforcement, and depression, but also includes providing resources and opportunities for parents and youth (Shore, 2003). Although these types of prevention efforts are being implemented, interventions after violent death need to be available not only in the acute aftermath but also long afterward as adolescent survivors and their families continue to struggle with the ongoing effects.

Acute Aftermath

Crisis interventions, which usually occur soon after the death and/or violence, should be planned well in advance. All those involved in conducting the intervention should know the protocols and procedures for responding. Whether the crisis is due to a single death, such as that of a classmate killed in a motor vehicle accident, or multiple deaths due to mass violence, such as the Oklahoma City bombing or September 11, plans need to be established for how to respond to children, adolescents, and their families. There are organizations that can help schools and youth-serving programs prepare for crises and that follow specific crisis intervention protocols. Due to the prevalence of violence, most schools have crisis intervention plans and crisis response teams. However, if the school does not have a plan or if all teachers and staff are not aware of it, planning and training must occur. In addition, adults who work with youth groups that are not associated with schools, such as summer camps, church youth groups, after school programs, and youth detention centers, should become familiar with mental health services in their community that can assist in times of crises.

> For more information about responding in the acute aftermath of violent death and for organizations that provide resources regarding violent death, see Appendix A.

Providing Follow-up Services

A critical component of crisis intervention services is identifying those in need of additional mental health intervention and providing or securing follow-up services. Follow-up services need to be offered to all affected by the violent death such as children and adolescents, parents, teachers, and staff. Mental health follow-up intervention can entail a variety of services, including psychological assessment, individual and family counseling, group therapy and support, consultation, advocacy and support, education and information, referrals, and consultation. This manual provides a guide to three types of mental health interventions that can be used after violent death for adolescents, parents, teachers, and staff as a follow-up to an initial crisis intervention. The three types of interventions described in this manual include: a 10-week time-limited grief and trauma group for adolescents, a one-time educational parent group, and a one-time teacher and staff educational group.

Not all youth who have had someone close to them die due to violence will need mental health intervention. Indeed, many youth have strong support systems, personal strengths, and resources to assist them with coping with the death. However, this is not the case for all adolescents, and failing to provide intervention to those who do need it can be detrimental. Following are some indicators that an adolescent may need mental health intervention:

- Limited support
- Poor coping skills
- Experiencing traumatic reactions, such as intrusive death images or persistent avoidance of any reminders of the death or loss
- Negative attitude about life
- Academic decline (lasting more than 1 to 2 months)
- Depression (fatigue, sleep difficulties, appetite change, irritability)
- Talks or hints about wanting to die or has extreme fear of others dying
- Angry outbursts
- Loss of interest in activities once enjoyed
- Prior significant loss, trauma, and/or psychiatric problems
- Substance abuse
- Youth or guardian requests mental health intervention

Adolescents who are having suicidal thoughts need immediate intervention services. Also, adolescents indicating substance abuse should be referred for substance abuse treatment. After violent death, it is expected and normal that adolescents will be distressed and may exhibit a range of symptoms. It is important that all youth and their parents, teachers, and significant adults are educated about the effects of witnessing violent death, hearing about violent death, and/or having someone close die due to violence. Information should be provided about where and how adolescents can receive mental health services if they are needed immediately or in the future. Youth with past mental illness, trauma, loss, or abuse should be monitored closely and offered mental health intervention, if needed, as problems related to past experiences may resurface.

We cannot always rely on crisis interventions to identify youth who may need mental health assistance. Sometimes, crisis interventions don't occur at all, for example, when officials do not see them as necessary or know that a violent death has occurred. In other cases, when there is a crisis intervention, not all youth who may need assistance have been identified. Sometimes, months or years have passed since the violent death, and adults who are currently working with the youth may not know the youth's experience. In these cases, facilitators for the time-limited grief and trauma group may need to conduct outreach and screening to identify adolescents in need of mental health services (as discussed in chapter 14) and who may benefit from group intervention.

Why Group Work?

Whether group intervention is provided to adolescents who all have experienced the same violent death or to youth who have experienced the death of someone close who their peers did not know, many bereaved adolescents can benefit from a time-limited grief and trauma group intervention. This type of intervention is not considered crisis intervention, as it is not designed to meet the acute needs of youth immediately after violent death. However, when the initial shock abates (at least one month), some adolescents may benefit from participating in a time-limited grief and trauma group. For some adolescents, the initial and ongoing support of family, friends, religious leaders, and so on will be enough to help them cope with the aftermath. However, other youth, especially those who continue to experience traumatic symptoms associated with the violent death (see chapter 6), may need the additional support of the group intervention. The group model described in this manual may be used as a follow-up intervention after providing initial crisis intervention, or as the initial mental health intervention that the youth receives after the death.

The group model is designed to reduce traumatic reactions associated with the violent death, provide education about grief and trauma reactions, and provide a safe environment for the youth to share some of his/her thoughts and feelings surrounding the violent death and loss.

Purpose of Grief and Trauma Groups for Adolescent Survivors
The overall goal of this grief and trauma group model is to reduce traumatic symptoms associated with the violent death and assist with facilitating the grief process.

   Three main goals of the grief and trauma group:
   1. To reduce traumatic reactions associated with the violent death.
   2. To provide education about grief and traumatic reactions.
   3. To offer a safe environment for the youth to share some of his/her thoughts and feelings about the violent death and loss.

Who Should Participate?

The main criteria for participating in grief and trauma groups is that the adolescent has had someone close who has died due to violence and/or has witnessed violent death. The term "someone close" is to be determined by the youth. Being a "witness" not only includes watching the violent death but also seeing elements of the aftermath, such as the dead body, the wrecked cars, blood, or a bullet hole. It is anticipated that youth in the group will be experiencing some traumatic symptoms and grief reactions, and/or may be having some decline in their overall functioning. The time since the death should be at least 1 month. Both the youth and his/her guardians need to agree to participate. Youth who are experiencing extreme stress, debilitating psychiatric disorders resulting in very poor functioning, and/or who are having suicidal ideation should not participate in the group until they are stabilized. Also, youth who are abusing substances need to be referred to treatment. Once they are able to control their substance use, they can participate in the group. Further information about screening for group participation is discussed in chapter 14.

Benefits of Group Work With Adolescents After Death

There are numerous benefits for conducting time-limited group therapy with adolescents that may not be possible to accomplish in brief individual and family therapy. From a pragmatic standpoint, time-limited group intervention allows more youth to be seen. Also, it generally costs less than individual and family therapy. From a therapeutic standpoint, group intervention can offer some benefits that individual and family therapy may take longer to accomplish. There are limitations to group intervention, such as participants not getting the individual attention that they may need and issues that are not part of the group goals may not be addressed. Some youth may need other types of mental health intervention while they are participating in the group and some may need additional intervention after the group has ended.

The therapeutic benefits of time-limited group intervention are numerous. Group therapy allows for youth to see first hand that other youth are experiencing similar reactions after the violent death, which contributes to the normalization of the experiences. When youth are participating in therapy together, the stigma associated with seeing a mental health professional often decreases. They see that other youth are in the group and that they are not so different from them. Common benefits of bereavement groups for adolescents include: stigma and feelings of being different are decreased, helpful information about bereavement is provided, difficult feelings can be contained, and youth are encouraged to express emotions (Corr, Nabe, & Corr, 1997). This grief and trauma group model includes several other benefits as well.

This grief and trauma model attempts to teach the youth and raise their awareness of coping skills so that they may be able to better accommodate the violent death and loss. A main emphasis of the group format is to reduce traumatic reactions that may be interfering with the bereavement process. As part of the bereavement process, the adolescents are encouraged to share with others in the group memories about the person who died. In the group, adolescents are given permission to grieve, which is not always the message that they receive from their parents, peers, teachers, and other significant people. As youth share their experiences, education about grief and traumatic reactions is provided to help normalize the experience. Useful information that may pertain to the type of death is also provided. For example, youth who have had a friend die of suicide may want to know some of the factors that have been associated with teen death, or an adolescent who has a family member testifying in a homicide case may be provided with information about the criminal justice process, or an adolescent whose friend died in a drunk driving accident may want to know how he or she can get involved in drunk driving prevention efforts.

None of these benefits will be fully realized without a sense of safety and cohesion within the group. Therefore, significant emphasis is placed on making the group experience a safe one where adolescents feel respected and comfortable sharing their thoughts and feelings surrounding the death and loss, and about ongoing adjustments that they are having to make as a result of the violent death. In the context of sharing their thoughts and feelings, the group experience can help adolescents begin to explore the meaning of the loss in their lives. This will certainly take longer than

---

Benefits of Grief and Trauma Groups with Adolescents After Violent Death

1. Reduce traumatic reactions that may be occurring as a result of the violence and death.
2. Facilitate memories of the deceased.
3. Dispel the stigma of therapy and mental health intervention.
4. Decrease feelings of being different due to the violent death.
5. Provide education about grief and trauma.
6. Provide specific information related to the death such as information about suicide, criminal justice processes, violence prevention organizations, crime victim assistance resources.
7. Help with the containment of difficult feelings.
8. Assist with the expression of intense emotions.
9. Teach and raise awareness of coping skills to deal with the loss and violent death.
10. Normalize the experience of grief and traumatic reactions.
11. Give the adolescent permission to grieve.
12. Provide a safe place to share thoughts and feelings surrounding the death and loss.
13. Help the adolescent explore the meaning of the loss in his or her life.
14. Help the adolescent begin to construct a coherent story/narrative of what happened.
15. Help the adolescent make adjustments to the loss.
16. Explore current life decisions and future goals.

---

10 sessions, but it can be the beginning of trying to understand how the death and loss has affected them, who they are now and what they want for their future. Often before adolescents begin to struggle with the meaning of the violent death in their lives, they must first try to put together their story about what happened. The group model can help adolescents begin to construct a coherent story about the violent death and be able to share it with others without become completely

overwhelmed. Although it may be unrealistic to assume that all of these benefits can be completely realized within the 10-week time frame, the group experience can raise awareness for the participants of their coping skills. Future goals and ambitions also are explored and adolescents are encouraged to examine how some of their current life decisions may affect their future.

Efficacy of Time-Limited Grief and Trauma Groups for Adolescents after Violent Death

Research on the efficacy of group intervention with adolescents bereaved due to violence is relatively recent. However, there is empirical evidence to suggest that time-limited grief and trauma groups with adolescents who are witnesses of violent death and/or who have had someone close die due to violence is an effective intervention modality for reducing traumatic stress. Because of limitations in research methodology, questions such as what type of interventions work best and with what populations remain unanswered. All the studies reviewed in the following paragraphs used manualized interventions and standardized assessment scales. The number of group sessions provided ranged from 4 to 20 and some group models included individual sessions. The dropout rates ranged from zero (Saltzman, Pynoos, Layne, Steinberg, & Aisenberg, 2001) to 18% (Pfeffer, Jiang, Kakuma, Hwang, & Metsch, 2002). Sample sizes in these studies ranged from 17 (March, Amaya-Jackson, Murry, & Schulte, 1998) to 45 (Salloum, Avery, & McClain, 2001), and included youth from various racial/ethnic and income groups. The time since the death ranged from 1 month to 10 years and the types of violent deaths and relationships to the deceased varied. Some of the studies had control groups and comparison groups.

The grief and trauma group format presented in this manual has been adopted from a model that was used in a pilot study (Salloum, Avery, & McClain, 2001). Forty-five low-income inner-city African-American adolescents between the ages of 11 and 19 participated in six school-based grief and trauma groups. All of the adolescents had someone close die due to homicide. The time since death ranged from 1 month to 10 years, with an average of 2 years at intervention. Attrition was 17.8%, with four main reasons for dropping out: ran away from home; truant, changed schools, or was suspended; hospitalized for medical condition; and parents revoked consent. Study results indicated an overall significant decrease in traumatic symptoms. Symptom clusters in the areas of reexperiencing and avoidance were significantly decreased. Although there was a decrease in hyperarousal symptoms, it was not significant. The authors suggest that with adolescents continuing to live in violent environments, amidst constant fears and threats, the model may need to include additional relaxation and self-calming activities. The authors also suggested that interventions must occur at the macro level with policies and communities creating safer environments. There were several limitations cited in the pilot study, including weak sampling methods, lack of a control or comparison group, and small sample size (Salloum, Avery, & McClain, 2001). However, this pilot study contributes to the evidence that time-limited grief and trauma groups are an effective approach for helping adolescents after violent death.

March, Amaya-Jackson, Murry, and Schulte (1998) conducted one of the first controlled studies of a protocol driven, time-limited cognitive-behavioral group treatment for children and adolescents (age 10 to 15) suffering from posttraumatic stress disorder (PTSD) resulting from a single-incident trauma. Several of the participants were also suffering because of the death of someone close. This 18-week group intervention included a "pull-out session" during the tenth session, which focused on identifying trauma reminders, recounting the traumatic narrative, and correcting misattributions and distortions. At the end of the intervention 57% (8 of 14 children) no longer had PTSD, and at a 6-month follow-up 86% (12 of 14) were free of PTSD. Anxiety, depression, and anger also decreased. As the authors continue to test the generalizability of this protocol, a grief component has been added for participants struggling with grief issues and the intervention has been shortened to 12 sessions (March, Amaya-Jackson, Murry, & Schulte, 1998).

In another study (Goenjian et al., 1997), a school-based treatment was provided to 35 early adolescents about a year and a half after the 1988 Armenian earthquake where thousands of people were killed and children and adolescents witnessed extreme destruction. The adolescents participated in a 6-week structured protocol consisting of four 30-minute classroom group psychotherapy sessions and two 1-hour individual psychotherapy sessions. The main goal of the intervention was to decrease posttraumatic stress and depression. A group of 29 children who lived in the same area as the children in the study and who experienced the devastation caused by the earthquake were used as a comparison group. At posttest, the intervention group reported significant decrease in posttraumatic stress symptoms in all three categories: intrusion, avoidance, and arousal; and no change in depression scores. However, the adolescents without the intervention reported an increase in scores over time in posttraumatic stress and depression. Goenjian and associates (1997) suggest that the worsening of symptoms among the nonintervention group may have been due to constant traumatic reminders, such as destroyed buildings, for which they did not receive treatment to reduce their reactivity. Furthermore, the authors note that despite the significant decrease in posttraumatic stress symptoms, the adolescents who participated in group still exhibited moderate symptoms and might have benefited from more sessions, different interventions, or booster sessions.

Saltzman, Layne, Pynoos, Steinberg, and Aisenberg (2001) designed a school-based trauma and grief-focused group intervention that consists of twenty 50-minute sessions, which focus on building group cohesion, strengthening coping skills, processing the traumatic experience, and promoting adaptive grieving and normal development. In their study, 26 students (11 to 14 years old, 68% Hispanic, 28% African American, and 4% Caucasian) who had experienced one or more significant traumas or losses, such as assault or death of a parent, and who were experiencing clinically significant stress, grief, or impaired functioning, participated in the intervention. At posttest, posttraumatic stress scores significantly decreased and grade point averages improved, but there was no significant difference in pre-post depression scores. In addition to these findings, the youth who reported loss histories (7 of 26) reported significant pre- to post-decrease in complicated grief symptoms. None of the youth dropped out of the group intervention. There may be several factors that contributed to the success of no dropouts, such as the pre-group screening consisted of referring some youth to individual counseling and selecting only those who: had experienced the trauma or loss more than three months prior, did not have severe trauma or grief, wanted to be in the group, and were stable and safe (Saltzman, Pynoos, Layne, Steinberg, & Aisenberg, 2001).

In 2002, Pfeffer, Jiang, Kakuma, Hwang, and Metsch compared outcomes of children (age 6 to 15) who had and had not received a time-limited manual-based group intervention to improve the mental health of suicide-bereaved children. The children (mostly white middle class) were divided into groups of similar ages. The intervention consisted of developmentally specific sessions based on attachment theory, responses to loss, and cognitive coping. Issues surrounding suicide, such as defining suicide, reasons people commit suicide, and suicidal urges, were discussed along with supportive activities that facilitated expressions of grief. The intervention consisted of a

10-week (90 minutes each week) psychoeducational and support group for the children and a concurrent group for the parents. The objective of the intervention was to reduce anxiety, depression, and posttraumatic stress symptoms and to improve social adjustment in suicide-bereaved children. Results revealed that the children who participated in the intervention had a significant decrease in anxiety and depression and there was a trend of lower posttraumatic stress symptoms. There were no significant differences in outcome scores for social adjustment. Depression among parents also was measured pre- and post- and there was no difference in scores. However, the parent group did not specifically focus on the parents' grief or depression but, rather, on ways for them to help their children cope. Although this control group study is a major contribution to exploring the efficacy of time-limited groups for children after violent death, the dropout rate is a concern. The dropout rate for children assigned to the intervention group was 18% (24 remaining) and the dropout rate for children assigned to the control group was 75% (nine remaining) (Pfeffer, Jiang, Kakuma, Hwang, & Metsch, 2002). The reasons for dropping out may provide clinical insight into different approaches to serving this population. Dropouts for the intervention group occurred only while the children were waiting for the group to begin. This may suggest that once screened, intervention needs to begin immediately as it may be too anxiety-provoking to wait. The families receiving intervention reported that they did not return for post-assessment because they had difficulty keeping appointments (55%) or they did not want to talk about the death (45%). Similarly, the nonintervention children reported that they dropped out because they were too busy to schedule appointments (66%), did not want to talk about the loss (20%), or sought intervention elsewhere (20%). Whereas children in both intervention and nonintervention groups cited "not wanting to talk about the loss" as a reason for dropping out (Pfeffer, Jiang, Kakuma, Hwang, & Metsch, 2002), there was a time when they had consented to participate. Perhaps if the intervention had started immediately after the consent they would have not dropped out. Further, with more than 50% in both groups indicating difficulty keeping appointments, community-based groups in which children and adolescents gather (school, church, community center) may have made it easier to attend the group.

Grief and trauma group models have also been specially designed to use with incarcerated youth (Rynearson, Favell, Belluomini, Gold, & Prigerson, 2002). In a juvenile detention center, 40 youth participated in a 10-week-session (90 minutes each week) group intervention aimed at reducing distress related to the violent death of a friend or family member. The average time since the death was 2.5 years. Most of the youth were involved in another type of psychiatric treatment as 66% had a psychiatric disorder. The dropout rate was 10%. At the end of the intervention, there was a significant decrease in depression, traumatic stress, and grief reactions (Rynearson, Favell, Belluomini, Gold, & Prigerson, 2002).

Group facilitators must take great care when working with adolescents who have witnessed violence and experienced the death of someone close. It is important to use interventions that have shown some promising results and to continue to evaluate every group intervention (as discussed in chapter 14). Facilitators' work with adolescents must be based on evidence, theory, and practice experience in an effort to provide the most effective service and certainly to "do no harm." Researchers are currently conducting studies with children and adolescents after violent death and group facilitators must keep abreast of new research. Research also can be useful for group facilitators who may be seeking funding to support group services, as often funders want to know what evidence exists that the intervention is effective. Facilitators seeking funding to offer group intervention for youth who may not be able to afford mental health services may use the studies cited in this review as some support that time-limited grief and trauma groups have shown promising results in reducing distress in youth after violent death.

Adolescent Bereavement

What Are Bereavement, Mourning, and Grief?

The terms bereavement, mourning, and grief have been defined in many ways (e.g., see McNeil, 1997) and are often used interchangeably. In this manual, bereavement is used as an umbrella term that encompasses the entire process experienced by a survivor after a significant death/loss. Mourning is defined as the cultural expression of grief including social rituals, expressions, and customs. Grief is defined as the psychological, behavioral, and physiological reactions experienced by a survivor after a significant death/loss.

Adolescence

Adolescence is thought of as the time period between the ages of 10 and 20 years. Because this is such a wide range, adolescence is generally divided into three time periods: early (10–13), middle (14–16), and late (17–20) adolescence. There are often great differences between the ages. For example, "picture an eleven-year-old standing next to a nineteen-year-old, and you will quickly realize the extent of change over this period, as well as some of the distinctions from one period to the next" (Petersen & Leffert, 1995, p. 4). Scholars have assigned different ages to different time periods of adolescence, making it difficult to compare the stages. Therefore, the age assignments used in this manual are rough estimates and the term adolescent refers to a person between 10 and 20 years of age. This range can present a serious concern for group facilitators who are not familiar with changes that occur during adolescence and who are not sensitive to the various needs of different ages (further discussion about the requirements for group facilitators can be found in chapter 13).

Despite the widespread notion that adolescence is a time of tremendous stress and turbulence, most adolescents fare quite well. However, adolescence is a time when the most difficulty in one's life is likely to arise (Arnett, 1999). Developmental transitions are occurring in multiple areas such as biological changes, cognitive changes, and psychosocial development such as identity and relationships. These changes occur within the context of an adolescent's family, culture, peer group, neighborhood, school, and the broader society, all of which can have significant influence on the adolescent's development. When adolescents experience a death or witnesses violent death, strain on their development may occur. If their families and environments are also affected by the death, this can have a serious impact on their transitions of development (Petersen & Leffert, 1995).

Adolescent Bereavement

For adolescents, the intensity of the reaction to loss may be greater than adults (Harris, 1991; Meshot & Leitner, 1993) and "the circumstances of a violent death can be more difficult for an adolescent to understand than any other form of death" (Clark, Pynoos, & Goebel, 1996, p. 124). During the developmental stage of adolescence, the death of a significant person may cause difficulty with achieving autonomy, mastery, competency, control, and intimacy, all of which are important developmental tasks of this period (Corr, Nabe, & Corr, 1997). Because there are so many variables and influencing factors with adolescent development, it is difficult to make definitive statements about adolescents' adjustment after violent death. However, theory and research provides us some insight into the additional challenges that death places on adolescents.

In one of the largest studies with parentally bereaved children and adolescents (125 children ranging in age from 6 to 17), Worden and Silverman (1996) found that the bereaved children as compared to nonbereaved children had higher levels of social withdrawal, anxiety, and social problems, and lower self-esteem and self-efficacy. However, although most children did not show major signs of serious emotional and behavioral disturbances, there was a significant percentage of children with serious problems 1 year after the death (19%) and at 2 years (21%). For some children, some symptoms such as anxiety did not emerge until 2 years after the death. It is to be noted that most of the participants in this study (88.6%) had a parent die due to natural causes, whereas only 11.4% died from violent deaths (accidents, suicide, and homicide). An analysis between the differences of children and adolescents bereaved from natural death versus violent death was not conducted with this study. However, it seems that some important general clinical implications can be derived from this study for working with adolescents bereaved from violent death. First, some bereaved adolescents may not experience severe psychological problems as a result of a death of a parent and may not need therapeutic intervention. However, as discussed in chapter 1, early identification of youth in need of services should be conducted. Second, for adolescents who do experience significant emotional and behavioral problems, symptoms may last quite some time or may be revealed after months have passed. Therefore, for those adolescents who received therapeutic intervention after a death, follow-up services need to be made available. Furthermore, intervention services must be available to bereaved youth regardless of the amount of time that has passed since the death, as new issues that need intervention may emerge long after the death and loss.

Silverman and Worden (1992) also found that 4 months after the death of a parent, 61% of 125 children and adolescents reported experiencing some type of illness since the death (Silverman & Worden, 1992). It is important that youth be encouraged to practice good health when grieving, such as exercising, eating healthily, limiting caffeine, and getting enough sleep.

Gender differences in bereaved adolescents may depend on several factors, such as the development of the youth, culture, sex role expectations, relationship to the deceased, and gender of the youth and deceased. Statements about gender and bereavement are presented here as common responses and are in no way universal. They should be used with great caution. Some authors (Crenshaw, 1996) have reported that bereaved adolescent males tend to behave more aggressively, frequently challenging authority. They also may increase their use of alcohol and drugs. Males may be less likely than females to talk with their friends and family members about the death (Silverman & Worden, 1992). Bereaved adolescent females may overtly express their need for comfort and reassurance, and may seek comfort and consolation. Bereaved females may cry more than males (Meshot & Leitner, 1993). However, these reactions may change as the adolescent matures. For example, Worden and Silverman (1996) found that when they compared the reactions of adolescent boys (12 to 18) at 2 years versus 1 year to a nonbereaved control group, over time the bereaved adolescents became more withdrawn and had more social problems. Bereaved adolescent girls (12 to 18), when compared to a nonbereaved control group, did not show any differences at 1 year or at 2 years.

Whether the death is of a parent, sibling, relative, or friend, it is important to understand the meaning of that loss for the individual adolescent. For example, Podell (1989) states, "The traumatic loss of a peer cannot be taken at its face value, but needs to be comprehended in light of the specific meaning of the loss for each adolescent" (p. 65). We must not assume the closeness of the relationship based on the label assigned without exploring with the adolescent who that person was in their life. For example, a youth may report that their "aunt" died and may not state, unless asked, that his aunt raised him since he was 2 years old and he considers her his mother.

Sometimes youth will need permission to stop grieving. At a certain point it is healthy for the adolescent to resume normal activities. They may need adults to assure them that it is okay and not a sign of disrespect for the deceased (Crenshaw, 1996). If adolescents do not feel comfortable with receiving help from adults, they may find it useful to be in a support group with peers with similar experiences (Corr, Nabe, & Corr 1997; Corr, 1995).

Typically, adolescents need to feel that they fit in with their peers since socialization and peer support is an important part of adolescence. If the adolescent feels set apart from peers because of the loss, they may be very hesitant to express their grief. However, if the adolescent feels support from his or her peers during this time, it can be very consoling and comforting (Crenshaw, 1996). Research (Hogan & DeSantis, 1994; Schachter, 1991) suggests that peer support is one of the main sources of help for bereaved adolescents. However, not all adolescents will find peers to be helpful. Some adolescents have reported that they think some of their peers do not know how to respond and some act insincerely (Balk, 1983). Also, some adolescents may not share their grief with their peers as a way to guard themselves against the pain or for fear of overwhelming their friends (Harris, 1991).

Early Adolescence

Younger adolescents who have had a parent die may not be as independent as older adolescents and may have intense yearnings for parental nurturance. In addition, because they may not be able to leave the home as frequently as older adolescents, they remain surrounded by reminders of loss. It may be that younger adolescents have fewer resources than older adolescents to cope with the death and loss (Harris, 1991). Younger adolescents may have an extreme need for controlling their emotions in public. Such intense emotions may be expressed in private with the use of diaries, poetry, and writing. Peers and activities are often necessary distractions from the home. Younger adolescents who have had a parent or a significant adult figure die may mourn the loss of a role model who would have guided and taught them about socialization. Such a loss affects their developing identity. Christ (2000) has characterized early adolescent bereavement as a time of the coexistence of contradictory developmental tasks such as dependence-independence, detachment-attachment, emotional control-emotional explosions. To further complicate these tasks, this is a time when biological, cognitive, emotional, and social developments are all rapidly changing.

Middle Adolescence

Although middle-aged adolescents may be able to better tolerate intense feelings associated with grief than younger adolescents, they may find themselves coping by externalizing these feelings into episodes of drinking alcohol, testing limits with parents, having anger tantrums, and avoiding responsibilities at home. If a parent has died, they may have a more internalized image of the parent, which can assist them in coping but potentially cause more pain as they may feel like a part of them is missing (Christ, 2000). Arnett (1999) suggests that middle adolescence may be a time when adolescents experience more extreme and volatile moods. Death of someone close during this period may greatly intensify and depress the youth's mood. Although biology may play a significant role in mood disruption, the adolescent's capacity for abstract thinking also can affect how they perceive their situation, which in turn can significantly influence their mood (Arnett, 1999). Abstract thinking also allows adolescents to consider all aspects of the violent death. In their analysis of the violent death, they may consider their own actions and the actions of others, which may lead them to find people and sources to blame for allowing the death to occur. Their own feelings of guilt may intensify as well.

Late Adolescence

Older adolescents may be able to occupy themselves with activities outside the family, such as work or time with peers, which provide them a temporary escape. However, attention diverted elsewhere may contribute to denial and avoidance and prolong the grief process. Furthermore, if older adolescents seek support in relationships outside the home, such as with a boyfriend or girlfriend, and that relationship becomes strained, the adolescent may be left particularly vulnerable (Harris, 1991). If a parent dies, older adolescents may be expected to assume many of the parenting roles for younger siblings. Although this may create a sense of purpose for some, for others it may cause additional stress.

During late adolescence, rates of behaviors such as crime, substance use, risky automobile driving, and risky sexual behavior peak (Arnett, 1999). Not all adolescents in this time period engage in these risk behaviors. However, for those adolescents who are engaged in these activities or are at risk for engaging in these behaviors, having someone close die due to violence or witnessing a violent death may increase the risky behavior or likelihood that the adolescent becomes involved in these types of behaviors.

The Bereavement Process

In an effort to understand the bereavement process, scholars and practitioners have proposed various theories, stages, tasks, and models. It should be noted that these perspectives are influenced and biased by those who develop them, those who are studied, past history, and the prevailing culture. However, despite these limitations, most practitioners would agree that practicing with bereavement theory helps make meaning of the process and guide the intervention. Experienced practitioners understand that not all bereaved individuals will fit the theory. Indeed, most times, bereavement does not follow an orderly process nor does it have a distinct ending point. Nevertheless, it is useful for practitioners to have an underlying theory of bereavement when working with the bereaved while always remaining focused on the individual's unique experience.

In this time-limited grief and trauma model, the three psychological tasks developed by Baker, Sedney, and Gross (1992) are used to guide the sessions. The ordering of these tasks are congruent with group theory (as discussed in chapter 5) which was also included in designing the group model. Chapter 16 provides a chart that displays the tasks of bereavement, stages of group development and the corresponding group topics and activities. This psychological phase-tasks framework was chosen over other useful bereavement models (e.g., Worden, 1996), because it includes aspects that will help youth who are experiencing traumatic responses as well as grief and it specifically addresses developmental concerns. As with other bereavement models, Baker and associates recognize that psychological tasks may be accomplished in a nonlinear fashion and over time. Also, task completion is dependent on developmental and environmental factors and death-related factors such as the significance of the loss. The three psychological tasks are described in terms of early, middle, and late bereavement tasks.

Tasks of Bereavement

Early-Phase Tasks: Understanding and Self-Protection

The early tasks are centered on attempting to understand what has happened while protecting one's self from the full emotional impact. During this task, safety needs to be established, information needs to be provided about the death, and coping mechanisms that provide protection from the potential devastating impact need to be employed (Baker, Sedney, & Gross, 1992). In the group, establishing a sense of safety must be the priority in the beginning and it needs to be maintained throughout the sessions. Without a sense of safety, it may be difficult for adolescents to begin to talk about the death and loss. Most adolescents in the group will have a "story" about what happened, although sometimes information may have been withheld from the youth by the family. In these cases, youth often fill in the gaps. If there is missing information, youth often continue to search for details. However, even when the youth knows what happened, violent death is difficult to understand. Youth may never truly understand what happened, as many facts surrounding the death may be unknown or just not make sense. However, it is important that they are eventually able to construct a narrative about the death and tolerate sharing this with others in the group without experiencing severe distress. Having youth tell who died and how is only briefly addressed in the first two sessions and group members are given choices about what they would like to share.

Self-protective factors such as denial, avoidance, distraction, humor, or being withdrawn are utilized during this stage. These factors are to be respected in the group as the youth may use these as strategies to avoid becoming too overwhelmed. These coping techniques may also be used until the adolescent progresses and realizes that they can tolerate being in the group and that it is safe to share their emotions. If group members' self-protective strategies are not allowed to be utilized to some degree in the beginning of the group, members may become aggressive, withdrawn, or drop out (Baker, Sedney, & Gross, 1992). To help members ease their defenses and understand their own reactions, it is important to provide education and normalization about grief and trauma, which is addressed in the second and third sessions.

Middle-Phase Tasks: Acceptance and Reworking

Baker, Sedney, and Gross (1992) identify three tasks of the middle phase: acknowledging the reality of the loss, reevaluating the relationship to the deceased, and tolerating psychological pain that accompanies the realization of the loss. For adolescents who have the cognitive ability to understand that death is final, they may still need time to understand the finality. The constant absence of the deceased may thrust the loss into every aspect of the youth's life. When the deceased is someone with whom the adolescent shared a close bond, discovering ways to remain connected in order to continue the relationship in a different manner may be the task at hand. During this phase, painful feelings may emerge, such as ambivalence, anger, guilt, and abandonment. For adolescents after violent death, these feelings may be complicated by traumatic reactions. How the youth tolerates and copes with this phase will depend on their developmental capacity and supportive environment. Younger adolescents may take longer with this phase since tolerating such pain may be endured in short timeframes. However, for all youth this phase usually requires some time, as there are often many feelings to sort through and painful adjustments in life to be made.

To assist the group members during this stage, session 4 explores losses in the youths' life and focuses on coping strategies to address loss. Sessions 5, 6, and 7 recognize traumatic reactions and intense feelings that may arise and techniques to tolerate and manage the responses are addressed. In an effort to help youth stay in control, ways to create a sense of safety are explored and relaxation techniques are utilized.

Youth in the group who have had someone close die more than a year ago may know all too well that all of these feelings rarely disappear after 10 sessions. However, it is hoped that youth can learn to tolerate these feelings, and find constructive ways to handle them. It is also hoped that with active coping these feelings will decrease in intensity. Furthermore, the intent is that when these reactions resurface in the future (hopefully to a lesser degree) they will not cause significant impairment in functioning. During the middle phase, it is acknowledged that there will be times, such as anniversary dates, holidays, and other important times in the youth's life, when these feelings will emerge. Such occurrences have been described as subsequent temporary upsurges of grief (STUG) (Rando, 1993). The prediction of STUGs, along with exploring ways to cope in the future, may help the youth cope when these occur.

Late-Phase Tasks: Identity and Development

Baker, Sedney, and Gross (1992) identify several tasks to be addressed in this phase: integrate the loss into one's identity, engage in healthy relationships, internalize an ever-changing representation of the deceased, resume with developmental tasks and employ coping strategies when upsurges of grief (or STUGs) occur. This phase is open-ended and becomes a part of the youth's developmental course.

The salience of the tasks in this phase may depend in large part on what role the deceased played in the adolescent's life. If the deceased did, or if the youth had hoped the deceased would, play a large role in shaping the youth's identity, this task may take some time. The youth will need to find ways to integrate into their identity who the deceased was to them without having their self concept become completely overshadowed by the deceased. Sometimes, youth may be reluctant to engage in new relationships or to invest in old ones for fear that they will be abandoned again. Bereaved adolescents will need to reengage with others without constantly becoming upset by the realization that the relationship is not like the one they had with the deceased. As previously discussed, if the deceased was a significant person with whom the adolescent shared a close bond, it may be helpful for the adolescent to remain connected with the deceased in a manner that allows the relationship to change as the youth matures so that it can fulfill different needs.

Sometimes, bereaved youth find that due to the bereavement process and all of the changes that have occurred in their lives since the death, they have stopped engaging in developmental tasks and activities that are typical of adolescents. Although the violent death may certainly lead them down a different path than perhaps they were headed, it is important for youth to resume an appropriate developmental course (Baker, Sedney, & Gross, 1992). This may be difficult for some adolescents since they may receive new messages, such as they have to grow up now (Silverman & Worden, 1992) or they have to take care of their siblings.

For bereaved youth who are experiencing traumatic reactions, the trauma may affect their development course. If an adolescent does not see a future for him or herself, they may have little motivation to resume or partake in present and future-oriented activities. The youth's attitude toward life may have been extremely altered by the violent death and the youth may skip the tasks of adolescence and engage in adult activities (Pynoos & Nader, 1988). Youth should be encouraged to delay major life decisions until the intensity of the traumatic and grief reactions subside. It is important for these youth to understand the connection between their new attitude and the violent death (Pynoos & Nader, 1988). Moreover, youth need to have a sense of purpose and meaning in their life. As Garbarino (1999) explains, trauma can cause two types of wounds: psychological trauma, such as posttraumatic stress, and philosophical trauma. Philosophical trauma is the "wound of meaninglessness" (p. 58) and " ... if one can heal from or avoid ... the wound of meaninglessness, one can likely deal with the first wound ... " of psychological trauma

(Garbarino, 1999, p. 158). If all of the other tasks, such as integrated self-identity, healthy relationships, utilization of healthy coping strategies, and an internalized representation of the deceased (which provides guidance, comfort, and a sense of connections), are accomplished in this late phase, the wound of meaningless can be avoided. If not, helping the youth to find meaning in his or her life should be the number one focus in this late phase task.

Sessions 8, 9, and 10 address some of these late phase tasks. Session 8 includes a discussion of supports. Adolescents are encouraged to identify significant people who are helpful to them and to talk about the different roles they play in their life. If the violent death affected their family members, the activity is to explore the affects on different family members. Hopefully by understanding the changes in other family members and being able to talk about their own loss, they will be better able to communicate with bereaved family members. Sometimes in the context of discussing spirituality, the topic of maintaining connections is addressed as youth may talk about souls, spirits, and connecting experiences with the deceased. Also, adolescents are encouraged to identify what is meaningful in their lives. Reviewing coping strategies again can raise awareness of ways to cope with STUGs. Aspects of identity after the death and one's developmental path are addressed by evaluating the group's goals, exploring how the adolescent has changed and discussing future short-term and long-term goals.

Stages of Group Development

Group facilitators must be knowledgeable about stages of group development and group dynamics. The following section is provided as an overview and reminder of aspects of group development. Group stages can influence the process and content of the sessions and the tasks that are to be accomplished. However, because there are so many unique factors involved with the group members and the group, the stages of group development may vary significantly from group to group (Northen & Kurland, 2001).

Although numerous scholars have proposed different theoretical group stage models (Tuckman, 1963; Northen & Kurland, 2001; Yalom, 1995) most would agree that there is a beginning, middle, and end, and that often conflict or tension and cohesion are two elements that occur during the development of the group. As the group progresses through these stages, the tasks to be completed and the behaviors of the group members change. There is often overlap between the transitions but during each stage certain themes and tasks become predominant (Northen & Kurland, 2001). Hellen Northen, an expert on group work since the 1960s, developed a four-stage model which focuses on the socioemotional themes in the development of group work and corresponding tasks. The four stages are orientation-inclusion, uncertainty-exploration, mutuality-goal achievement, and separation-termination.

As the time-limited grief and trauma group in this manual is structured according to the three tasks of bereavement (as discussed in chapter 4), it also takes into consideration the four stages of group development. The progression of the tasks of bereavement and the stages of group development are such that similar themes, dynamics, and tasks are addressed relatively at the same time. Chapter 16 provides a chart that presents the tasks, stages, and group topics.

During the early tasks of bereavement—understanding and self-protection—the first two stages of group development (orientation–inclusion and uncertainty–exploration) are progressing. As the middle phase of bereavement—acceptance and reworking—occurs, the group stage of mutuality-goal achievement occurs. At the end of the group, the late tasks of bereavement—identity and development and separation-termination—are taking place simultaneously. As already stated, this is theoretical and not every group will proceed accordingly, but the model has been developed with bereavement theory and group theory in mind as well as with knowledge about trauma and grief.

Orientation–Inclusion

In the first stage of group development, orientation–inclusion, themes of inclusion and dependence are present and the main task is to become oriented about the purpose, roles, and expectations of the group (Northen & Kurland, 2001). Because the group members may not know or trust one another, they may depend on the group leaders to provide guidance. In the first couple of group meetings, the facilitators need to actively lead the sessions. Group members may be ambivalent about continuing. Youth with high levels of uncertainty and anxiety about participating in the group are at risk for dropping out and need to be provided with a tremendous amount of support and assurance.

In the beginning and throughout the group, individual members may take on certain roles. Some roles, such as the group clown, may help the group with reducing anxiety. However, the facilitators want to make sure that members do not get stereotyped in a way that does not allow them to meet their own goals. For example, the clown at times needs to be able to be serious and the group needs to be able to accept that expression as well. When potentially negative roles are being formed, such as the bully, facilitators need to be assertive in redirecting interactions that lessen the behaviors. Some strategies include using support and empathy, approving of behaviors that should be the norm, focusing on common feelings of group members, involving certain members who need to be included in the group in a positive way, setting firm limits to define acceptable behavior, and helping members to solve conflicts (Northen & Kurland, 2001).

In the first session, group leaders acknowledge the commonality of experiences of violence and death. They need to try to make the youth feel at ease and like they "fit in" with their peers. Also, clear messages that differences are to be expected and respected must be conveyed. Because some members may be reluctant to share personal information, confidentiality is stressed and all members must sign a contract to maintain it. The group facilitators explain the structure of the group and what is to be expected of the members. To lessen the fear of adolescents that they may become too overwhelmed, facilitators need to communicate that they will try to follow the youth's pace in terms of how much or little they feel they can share, but that they encourage them to try to share as much as they feel they can. Facilitators announce that members do have the "right to pass" on speaking. For example, in a group with seven adolescents, two members did not want to share with the group who died. The facilitator replied by stating, "You have the right to pass, and we will respect that. Sometimes it can be very difficult to talk about these types of things, especially when you are with people whom you really don't know. Hopefully, as we spend more time together it will become easier and you can share with us more about your thoughts and feelings about what has happened." The adolescents should be praised and commended for attending the group. Also, it is important that facilitators offer some sense of hope in terms of letting them know that the group structure is designed to help them cope better with what has happened and that many youth, after completing the 10 sessions, have reported that it helped.

The second session includes education and normalization, which can help the youth understand their feelings and that they are not "crazy." The first drawing or writing activity occurs in the second session. Facilitators need to state that grammar and spelling are not important, although if participants want or need help the facilitators will help them. Also, the adolescents can choose between writing and drawing and can select which worksheet they want to complete. Allowing the youth the choices helps them to feel more in control, which is extremely important for youth after violent death. Most youth will participate in this activity since they work on it by themselves. However, some may still be hesitant to share with the other group members what they have written or drawn. For example, David, a 14-year-old boy whose cousin was murdered 1 year prior to the group, drew a very detailed picture of his cousin's death. Although David interacted and joked with other group members, when the facilitator asked members to share their drawings with the group, David turned his over and said, "No." The facilitator replied, "It is okay if you do not want to share it with us now. It can be very hard to talk about what happened and a lot of feelings can come up. I hope that eventually you and everyone in the group will be able to share not only what happened but also how you are feeling. When you are ready to share this with us, we will be ready to listen. When someone has died due to violence, one reaction is to try to avoid thinking about it. Avoidance is a common reaction to violent death." After the group, David stayed to help the facilitator put the chairs back in place. Without the facilitator asking, David showed the facilitator his drawing and said that he had talked with his cousin just before he was killed. The facilitator thanked him for sharing this with her and said that she hoped he would be able to share this with the group, too. The facilitator told him that she was looking forward to seeing him again at the next session.

Uncertainty–Exploration

The second stage of group development is called uncertainty–exploration. The main socioemotional themes are conflict and difference. With this stage, the main task is to develop trust, strengthen interpersonal relationships among group members, and help members understand expected benefits of group participation. As trust and cohesion begin to form, group members will begin to support each other, allowing the group's purpose to become a focus of the group (Northen & Kurland, 2001).

Uncertainty and tension during this stage is to be expected. Group members may become hostile toward the facilitators and test the limits and try to engage in power struggles. Clear limits, in a respectful manner, need to be set regarding what is allowed and what is not allowed. Slowly, as members become more comfortable, they will begin to engage more with each other, rather than with the facilitators. Hopefully, leadership and power will begin to shift to the group members. Also, group alliances may become more prevalent during this stage and facilitators, as in the first stage, need to continue to monitor and at times redirect these alliances and roles. During this stage, facilitators may begin to offer referrals to other resources that may benefit the participants and, if appropriate, help them with other concerns that may not be able to be addressed within the group. For example, mental health services may be provided to other family members, information about youth groups and/or prevention programs may be provided, or information about tutoring services may be offered for an adolescent whose grades have declined since the death.

Session 3 is an attempt to clarify the purpose of the group and the group goals and members are asked to sign a goal agreement form (see chapter 16, session 3). Members also can set any personal goals that they want to work on during the group. For example, David, who was always teasing others in the first two sessions, wrote that he wanted to work on "not kidding around in the group while in session." Hopefully, by this time the group members have become a little more comfortable with talking and participating in the group activities. For example, David shared with the other group members that he had talked with his cousin right before he died. He also shared with the group members his hope that his mother and father would get back together again (as they had recently divorced). Group facilitators need to continue to take an active role in coordinating the educational activity about grief and trauma until group members feel more comfortable in leadership roles and talking with each other.

In session 4, members discuss losses that have occurred in their lives and memories of the deceased. Confronting these realities of losses usually stirs many emotions, perhaps causing some members to reconsider their decision to be in the group. Facilitators need to take a leadership role to facilitate discussion and to raise awareness about coping strategies. Facilitators also need to encourage group members to talk with one another rather than only with them. Interaction among the members allows them to test trust and respect between them. When conflict occurs between group members, facilitators should encourage group members to problem solve and work it out as a group or between themselves, which can strengthen relationships. It is important that group members who may feel dissatisfied with the group experience or with the facilitators can express their concerns. Facilitators need to allow time for such dissatisfaction to be openly discussed and, when possible, addressed. Also, to address the distrust that group members may have toward the group facilitators, facilitators may want to raise the issue of existing differences that may cause barriers between the facilitators and group members such as age, race, culture, or experiences with violent death. Because of underlying fear and ambivalence about being in the group, members may complain about rather simple concerns. For example, several boys in a group complained because they did not have anything to drink with the snacks that were served. This can be easily taken care of by bringing drinks to the next group, which shows the members that their concerns are heard. However, when members direct their dissatisfaction toward a certain member in the group, this can be more difficult. Facilitators need to help the members see the commonalities among them and not allow any group member to be disrespected. When David and another boy in the group whom he had previously teased became upset with each other and stood up as if they were going to approach each other, the facilitator stood up, too, and stated, "We are not going to have this type of behavior in the group. Both of you need to sit down and take time to calm down. If you need to move away from each other to have space, go ahead." The facilitator moved two chairs for them to sit in which were far from each other. Both boys sat in the chairs. After about ten minutes, as the other group members worked in their books, the boys were ready to rejoin the group. The facilitator was then able to have them talk in a calm manner about what happened and the other group members were able to problem-solve with them.

Mutuality and Goal Achievement

In the third stage, mutuality and goal achievement, the socioemotional theme is intimacy and interdependency and the main task is goal achievement. By this time in the process of group development, members have learned they can accept and help each other. During this stage, cohesion, motivation, group attendance, group norms, goal clarity, trust, and empathy are all present, but there may be times of uncertainty and themes from the first two stages may resurface (Northen & Kurland, 2001).

With group members interacting more and being more intimate, members are able to learn more about themselves. This self-realization and acknowledgment of thoughts and feelings can be frightening for some members, but facilitators and group members can help the participants explore their feelings. There are numerous approaches that facilitators can use to help members with honest self-reflection. Strategies include supporting ventilation and naming the feelings, rephrasing statements to modify the way the adolescent looks at the situation, stating observations and encouraging members to see if these observations fit theirs, encouraging members to give each other feedback, using silence to promote reflection, conveying support, acceptance, and empathy, and using activities to help members to understand and express their thoughts and feelings. During this stage, which can be quite intense, facilitators need to respect members' needs to protect themselves and help members to manage overwhelming feelings. Facilitators may want to consider meeting individually with group members who do not seem to be participating in the group, or benefiting from it, to try to find out how to better meet some of their needs (Northen & Kurland, 2001).

The activities in sessions 5, 6, 7, and 8 challenge group members to express more of their thoughts and feelings about the death and loss. Session 5 focuses on identifying traumatic reactions and exploring ways to decrease these reactions. Having group members acknowledge traumatic reactions, which may not have been shared with other people, can help the members feel a certain connection with each other. However, the activity allows for an individualized exercise to address the member's unique experience, which provides for their individual needs to be met. At this point, it is hoped that members are beginning to trust each other more and trust the process of group as a means to help them. The topics (feelings, anniversaries, guilt, revenge, anger, spirituality, and family), which can be very personal, are purposely addressed during the goal stage so that members are able to be empathetic toward each other and mutually supportive. David shared in the group that he felt guilty about his cousin dying. He had wished that he was with his cousin and somehow thought if he were, he could have stopped it from happening. The facilitator and the other group members listened and then several of the boys told him that there was no way he could have known when he talked with his cousin what would happen the next day. Also, they challenged his belief that he could have prevented it. David also was able to share that he had been feeling very sad.

In bereavement groups, feelings may be discussed much earlier than in grief and trauma groups. Given that traumatic reactions may intensify feelings, grief and trauma group members need to feel safe, supported, and respected so that they can honestly address these feelings. Also, they need to have a sense of control and be able to use relaxation techniques to help them manage their thoughts and emotions.

Separation–Termination

Separation–termination is the fourth stage. The main socioemotional theme in this stage is separation, which involves ending and leaving the group. The tasks include completing unfinished business, reviewing progress, and helping members prepare for the future (Northen & Kurland, 2001).

In this stage, members experience another loss but have a chance to utilize their new coping skills. Group members and facilitators often have ambivalent feelings about ending. Members may not want to leave the newly formed peer support group and may protest by denying that the group is ending, missing sessions, or becoming angry with the facilitators or other group members. Facilitators need to acknowledge with the group members the difficulty with ending and the normal feelings that are surfacing. Group members must be given an opportunity to express their concerns and ambivalent feelings. An important activity during this stage involves reviewing and recognizing members' progress toward meeting the goals of the group and any individual goals. Some members may express that they are sad that the group is ending but also proud of what they have been able to accomplish and ready to move on. For members who did not meet their goals or who may need further services, information about additional resources and recommendations needs to be provided. As the group comes to an end, facilitators need to focus each adolescent on his or her future and help them to see hope ahead. Members are encouraged to use the skills they have learned in the group in their daily living (Northen & Kurland, 2001).

In the early sessions and at several points throughout the process, group members are reminded of the number of sessions that remain. The main focus of sessions 9 and 10 is separation and termination. Both of these sessions incorporate time to review individual member's progress. Evaluative posttests are administered to measure any changes and to assist the facilitator and youth in identifying difficulties and areas that the youth needs to continue to work on in the future. If group members were working on individual workbooks, they are given these to keep in the last session and encouraged to share their work with other significant people in their lives. If they did not finish the workbook, they are encouraged to complete this on their own while utilizing some of the skills they learned in the group. The activity in session 9 regarding future goals is essential. As discussed in chapter 4, issues of identity and the future are extremely important for adolescents after violent death. Session 10 involves a formal review process, which recognizes and celebrates the completion of the group. Members are given certificates of completion and may end the last group with a created ritual. At the end of the group, facilitators will complete an evaluation of each member's progress and provide additional resources, if needed. Facilitators will meet with any youth who was not able to make the last meeting in an effort to review progress, discuss feelings of ending, encourage continuation of learned coping strategies, and make recommendations if needed.

When David was asked to rank progress toward his goals, he circled 8 (with 10 being the highest) for learning more about grief and trauma, 9 for sharing some of his thoughts and feelings about what happened, and 10 for stopping kidding around while in session, although he changed this goal and said he learned how to "ignore ignorance." David's score on the posttest of traumatic stress indicated that he decreased 12 points but was still experiencing mild symptoms. At the end of the group, the facilitator recommended that David receive additional mental health intervention to address other unresolved issues about his family situation. David agreed to participate in individual counseling with the school social worker.

Posttraumatic Stress

It is important to be aware of the signs of posttraumatic stress, which may occur after a violent death, especially when the violence is witnessed. Adolescents should not suffer in silence and wonder, "what is wrong with me." Instead, education about common reactions needs to be provided. For youth whose traumatic symptoms have not lessened over time, interventions such as a grief and trauma group or other types of mental health services need to be available. Because traumatic symptoms can significantly impede the bereavement process (as discussed in chapter 7), information about posttraumatic stress is discussed in this chapter. The information about posttraumatic stress disorder is not provided so that group facilitators can diagnose group members. In fact, group facilitators should not diagnose group members with posttraumatic stress disorder, or any other type of psychiatric disorder, unless the facilitators have had appropriate training in assessment and diagnosis.

What Is Posttraumatic Stress Disorder (PTSD)?

Posttraumatic Stress Disorder, often called PTSD, is classified as a mental disorder that occurs as a result of an extreme stressor causing the person to respond with intense fear, helplessness, or horror. The extreme stressor or traumatic event can be experienced directly, witnessed, or learned about from the experience of others (*Diagnostic and Statistical Manual for Mental Disorders, fourth edition, text revised* [*DSM-IV-TR*], 2000). Some examples (*DSM-IV-TR*, 2000) of each type of exposure and extreme stressors are listed below:

- Experienced directly may include, but is not limited to, a severe automobile accident, terrorist attack, or natural or manmade disaster.
- Witnessing may include, but is not limited to, witnessing a violent death or unexpectedly witnessing a dead body or body parts.
- Learning about the experiences of others may include, but is not limited to, learning about a sudden unexpected death of a family member or close friend (*DSM-IV-TR*, 2000).

There are several criteria that need to be met for a person to be considered to have PTSD. The hallmark responses of PTSD include reexperiencing, avoidance, and numbing, and increased arousal. These responses must occur for more than 1 month and cause significant impairment in functioning (*DSM-IV-TR*, 2000). The following chart describes the number and types of symptoms required for meeting the criteria for PTSD.

According to the National Center for Post-Traumatic Stress Disorder (2003), PTSD is associated with neurobiological and physiological changes as well as with cooccurring psychiatric disorders such as major depression and substance use. Adolescents with PTSD often exhibit similar symptoms of adults with PTSD. However, adolescents are more likely to have difficulty with impulse control and may become more aggressive. Although younger children may reenact aspects of the traumatic event in their play, adolescents may incorporate aspects of the traumatic event into their daily activities, such as carrying a weapon (Hamblen, 2003).

Who Is More Likely to Develop PTSD?

Great caution must be exercised when using risk factors to determine the cause of PTSD as no one variable is likely to be the catalyst for developing the disorder. Although bereaved adolescents after violent death may experience posttraumatic symptoms, not all will meet the criteria for the diagnosis of PTSD. For example, in a sample of 138 youth who were friends of suicide victims, only 5% met the full criteria for PTSD (Brent et al., 1995).

Adolescents who witness the death or the aftermath and/or youth who experience a sense of threat associated with the violent death are at higher risk for developing posttraumatic stress. Also, the closeness of the relationship to the deceased victim may predispose youth to develop PTSD (Brent et al., 1995; Pynoos, Frederick, Nader et al., 1987). Furthermore, youth who have a history of substance abuse, mental illness, and/or suicide attempts are at greater risk for developing posttraumatic stress than those without such histories. Other factors that may increase posttraumatic stress include conflict in the family, concurrent depression, recent interaction with the deceased just prior to the death and guilt (Brent et al., 1995).

In a large longitudinal study (Giaconia et al., 1995), researchers examined the prevalence of PTSD, co-occurring disorders, and associated problems. Many of their findings were consistent with other studies. In their study with 384 adolescents, 43% of the adolescents reported experiencing a traumatic event by age 18 and 14.5% of these youth developed PTSD. Some of the most prevalent traumatic events included news of another's sudden death or accident, sudden injury or accident, and seeing someone hurt or killed. Although rape was not reported to be as prevalent as other traumas, youth who were raped (mostly females) were at the highest risk for developing PTSD. In this study, the rates of experiencing traumas were relatively equal among males and females. However, like other studies, females were more likely to develop PTSD. Nonetheless, the researchers suggest that even though the males did not report as many symptoms of PTSD as the females did, they remain at risk for developing problems in later adolescence (Giaconia et al., 1995). When a death occurs, the gender of the person who died in relation to the gender of the adolescent and the significance of the relationship may be associated with the link between gender and increased risk for PTSD. For youth with PTSD, there was a strong association between PTSD and substance dependence and major depression, which the researchers noted has been found in other studies. Furthermore, youth with PTSD had significantly more problems with interpersonal relationships, were at risk for suicidal thoughts and attempts, had poorer health, had lower grade

Diagnostic Criteria For Posttraumatic Stress Disorder

A. The person has been **exposed to a traumatic event** in which both of the following were present:
   1. The person experienced, witnessed, or was confronted with an event or events that involved actual or threatened death or serious injury, or a threat to the physical integrity of self or others.
   2. The person's response involved intense fear, helplessness, or horror. Note: In children, this may be expressed instead by disorganized or agitated behavior.

B. The traumatic event is **persistently reexperienced** in *one (or more)* of the following ways:
   1. recurrent and intrusive distressing recollections of the event, including images, thoughts, or perceptions. Note: In young children, repetitive play may occur in which themes or aspects of the trauma are expressed.
   2. recurrent distressing dreams of the event. Note: In children, there may be frightening dreams without recognizable content.
   3. acting or feeling as if the traumatic event were recurring (includes a sense of reliving the experience, illusions, hallucinations, and dissociative flashback episodes, including those that occur on awakening or when intoxicated). Note: In young children, trauma-specific reenactment may occur.
   4. intense psychological distress at exposure to internal or external cues that symbolize or resemble an aspect of the traumatic event.
   5. physiological reactivity on exposure to internal or external cues that symbolize or resemble an aspect of the traumatic event.

C. **Persistent avoidance** of stimuli associated with the trauma and numbing of general responsiveness (not present before the trauma), as indicated by *three (or more)* of the following:
   1. efforts to avoid thoughts, feelings, or conversations associated with the trauma
   2. efforts to avoid activities, places, or people that arouse recollections of the trauma
   3. inability to recall an important aspect of the trauma
   4. markedly diminished interest or participation in significant activities
   5. feelings of detachment or estrangement from others
   6. restricted range of affect (e.g., unable to have loving feelings)
   7. sense of a foreshortened future (e.g., does not expect to have a career, marriage, children, or a normal life span)

Diagnostic Criteria For Posttraumatic Stress Disorder (continued)

D. Persistent symptoms of **increased arousal** (not present before the trauma), as indicated by *two (or more)* of the following:
  1. difficulty falling or staying asleep
  2. irritability or outbursts of anger
  3. difficulty concentrating
  4. hypervigilance
  5. exaggerated startle response

E. Duration of the disturbance (symptom in Criteria B, C, and D) is **more than 1 month.**

F. The disturbance causes clinically significant distress or impairment in social, occupational, or other important areas of functioning.

  Specify if: **Acute:** if duration of symptoms is less than 3 months
              Chronic: if duration of symptoms is 3 months or more

  Specify if: **With Delayed Onset:** if onset of symptoms is at least 6 months after the stressor

Reprinted with permission from the Diagnostic and Statistical Manual of Mental Disorders, Fourth Edition, Text Revision. Copyright 2000 American Psychiatric Association.

point averages, and were at an increased risk for other mental health disorders than youth without PTSD (Giaconia et al., 1995). Given the high distress level, significant impairment, and associated problems related to PTSD, it is important to identify and provide intervention to youth who have PTSD and who are at risk for developing PTSD.

PTSD: General Guidelines For Practice

Usually, PTSD does not dissipate with the passage of time alone. Specific mental health interventions that have shown results in decreasing symptoms are often required for symptoms to lessen. Interventions, such as cognitive behavioral therapy, psychoeducation, parent involvement, play therapy, psychological first aid, 12-step programs (for adolescents with PTSD and substance abuse), eye movement desensitization and reprocessing, specialized interventions, and medications, have been effective in treating children and adolescents with PTSD (Hamblen, 2003). However, more research is needed to determine what types of interventions are best for which types of traumatic stressors (such as witnessing violent death or having someone close die due to violent death), with which populations, and for which types of symptoms and associated problems.

Some Factors Associated with Increased Risk for PTSD

Witnessing violence, violent dying, and/or aftermath

Perceived greater threat, fear, or danger

Closeness of the relationship to the deceased

Guilt or helplessness

Developmental status

Family discord

Prior history of suicide attempts

Parent/caretaker with PTSD or depression

Depression

Substance abuse

Prior history of mental illness

Prior abuse

Prior conflict with the deceased

Conflict between youth and parent

Limited support

Although several intervention approaches may be available to address PTSD, experts have set forth general practice parameters for treating children and adolescents with PTSD. Four main general practice parameters include: (1) exploring the trauma; (2) incorporating specific stress management techniques; (3) correcting inaccurate attributes; and (4) including parents (Cohen, 1998). All four of these guidelines are included to some extent in the grief and trauma group model used in this manual.

Exploration of the violent death and surrounding traumatic factors must be conducted in a manner that does not overwhelm the adolescent. Adolescents who participate in the screening process are provided the opportunity to talk about the traumatic death and some of the related disturbing factors. Also, in the first five sessions there are opportunities through different activities for youth to explore the death and loss. The use of stress management techniques such as deep breathing or invoking comforting memories of the deceased's life to counter the death narrative and imagery are important coping techniques when discussing the traumatic nature of the death and to help the adolescent deal with ongoing trauma and grief reactions. Sessions 4 and 5 specifically include stress management techniques. The group modality with peer discussion and facilitator guidance often provides an excellent opportunity for exploring and correcting distortions, such as thinking that one caused the death or could have stopped it from occurring or having survivor's guilt. The game *G.T. Cards,* which is played in the third session, includes statements designed to foster discussion about inaccurate attributes and negative cognitive changes that have occurred as a result of the violent death. If distortions are not adequately challenged, group facilitators may need to address them in another group session or individually with specific youth. While this grief and trauma group model does not specifically outline a simultaneous parent group, parent involvement in terms of psychoeducation is recommended (see chapter 11). Also, the eighth group session focuses on family adjustment and adolescents are encouraged to share some of what they have done in the group session with their parents.

What About Psychopharmacology?

Sometimes bereavement therapists and counselors who see grief as a normal process may be hesitant to refer bereaved adolescents for an evaluation for medication (Rando, 1992–1993). Similarly, trauma therapists may be hesitant to encourage an evaluation for psychiatric medication because this may pathologize the adolescent's "normal" response to an "abnormal event." However, for adolescents who may be too distressed to attend the group or whose PTSD symptoms are not decreasing with group intervention, facilitators should discuss with the parent or guardian and the adolescent a referral to a psychiatrist for medication. Such a referral may be necessary for adolescents who have preexisting psychiatric disorders or who are experiencing comorbid disorders such as depression, panic symptoms, or attention deficit hyperactivity disorder (Cohen, 1998; Rando, 1992–1993).

Responses to Youth Suffering from Posttraumatic Stress

Once a facilitator is aware that a young person is experiencing posttraumatic stress reactions, it is important that time is spent with the person to help them understand what they are experiencing (see chapter 14 for information about interviewing youth). Following are some examples of statements that facilitators may use when talking with youth:

- What you are experiencing is known as posttraumatic stress and the type of reactions that you have described occur to people who have experienced extreme stress, such as having someone close die or witnessing a violent death.

- Three common reactions of posttraumatic stress include reexperiencing, avoidance, and increased arousal (give examples of each). Unfortunately, these reactions usually do not just go away on there own, but we can work together so that you are not experiencing them as much. I realize that this may be hard and that you may want to just ignore that you are having these feelings or want to avoid ever talking about what happened, but know that we will go slowly and try to work together in a way where you do not feel too overwhelmed.

- Sometimes young people and adults drink alcohol or use substances as a way to numb the pain and to try to forget, but the fact is: It only makes it worse. It is important to let me know if you have used or start to use substances to try to deal with what is going on.

- Sometimes people who are experiencing posttraumatic stress have said that they feel depressed. Not all people, but some. Have you been feeling depressed lately? (Listen and respond.) If the youth does not know how to describe what he or she is feeling, consider asking the following questions. How have you been sleeping at night? How would you describe your energy level during the past 2 weeks: excellent, good, fair, or poor? Have you notice that you have been eating more or less? Have you been able to concentrate in school (or at your job)? Tell me about what you have done lately that you enjoyed. Have you ever had thoughts of wanting to hurt or kill yourself? (If yes, conduct an assessment of risk for suicide and/or refer immediately to a trained professional for an evaluation.)

- One of the most helpful things that you can do for yourself during this time is to take care of yourself and try to relax. While that may sound easy, I know that it can be hard sometimes. I would like to spend a few minutes and talk more about things you can do to take care of yourself and then I will share with you a relaxation technique that I want you to try (discuss with the youth healthy habits such as eating properly, getting enough sleep, limiting caffeine, and exercising, and then teach and do together a simple deep breathing exercise and/or muscle relaxation).

Traumatic Grief

Childhood traumatic grief is defined as "the impingement of trauma symptoms on the child's ability to appropriately mourn the loss of a loved one" (Cohen, Mannarino, Greenberg, Padlo, & Shipley, 2002, p. 308). Studies have shown that after death (Stoppelbein & Leilani, 2000) and after violent death (Nader, Pynoos, Fairbanks, & Frederick, 1990) children and adolescents have reported significant levels of posttraumatic stress. Whether an adolescent has had someone close to them die or witnessed or heard about a death, if the youth perceives the death as traumatic and has traumatic reactions, childhood traumatic grief may occur (Cohen et al., 2002).

With traumatic grief, both trauma and grief reactions are present, and the trauma symptoms interrupt or intensify the grief. Not all adolescents after violent death will experience traumatic grief. Some youth after violent death may experience only grief, whereas others may experience trauma and grief independently and still others may experience traumatic symptoms or posttraumatic stress disorder that is not interfering with the grief (Cohen et al., 2002).

Sometimes it may be difficult to distinguish between traumatic symptoms and grief reactions. However, when trauma and grief are both present, the symptoms that are common to each such as anxiety, irritability, emotional pain, loss of energy, sleep difficulty, difficulty concentrating, depression, and guilt may escalate (Nader, 1997). For example, "Anger commonly appears in the course of bereavement. Following trauma, it may be murderous rage" (Nader, 1997, p. 29).

The full criterion for PTSD does not have to be met for childhood traumatic grief to be present. However, there must be a significant presence of traumatic symptoms that directly affects the grief process. It is to be expected that immediately following a violent death some posttraumatic symptoms may be normative, but it is not expected that such symptoms will persist for months. For those youth who continue to have or who develop traumatic symptoms related to the death that significantly interfere with bereavement, traumatic grief is present (Cohen, Mannarino, Greenberg, Padlo, & Shipley, 2002). It is anticipated that as research continues a more complete definition of childhood traumatic grief with specific symptoms and duration will be developed.

Understanding Differences Between Trauma And Grief

Rynearson (2001) explains how the reactions from the traumatic nature of the death and from the loss are two distinct, but intertwined, distress responses. Both responses, traumatic distress and separation distress, are separated into specific thoughts, feelings, and behaviors. With trauma distress, the association is with reenactment, fear, and avoidance. The person becomes distressed by the replaying and/or the avoidance of the violent death. Separation distress occurs with thoughts of reunion, feelings of longing, and behaviors of searching. With violent dying, traumatic distress, which is often intense, takes precedence over separation distress and is frequently prolonged. When the traumatic distress begins to decrease, the separation distress gradually replaces it, which allows the bereaved to engage in the bereavement process without the constant interruption of traumatic reactions (Rynearson, 2001).

Raphael and Martinek (1997) provide an excellent explanation of the distinctions between traumatic reactions and bereavement reactions. In terms of cognitive processes, traumatic response would entail images of and preoccupations with the death, traumatically laden memories, including dreams, and reexperiencing threatening, fearful, or horrific aspects of the dying. Cognitive bereavement responses would be associated with images and preoccupations with the person being gone, memories of their life, and thoughts and sensations of the presence of the person.

The predominant affective reaction of traumatic stress is persistent anxiety caused by threat, danger, reminders, and intrusions about the death and surrounding circumstances. Anxiety, yearning, longing, and sadness may be present with affective bereavement reactions, but these emotions are primarily due to the reality of the loss of the person in the bereaved's life now and in the future (Raphael & Martinek, 1997).

The phenomena of avoidance may be evident in both traumatic reactions and bereavement reactions. However, people experiencing traumatic reactions may avoid any reminders (conversations, places, things, people) of the death, whereas avoidant bereavement reactions are concerned with avoiding reminders of the absence of the person. Similar to avoidance, both bereaved and traumatized people may experience arousal, but the arousal is caused by a different orientation. Traumatic reactions that include arousal stem from the threat and danger associated with the death, with the response being a hyperalertness. Arousal with bereavement is due to stimuli related to cues about the absent person and it is due to cues of the absent person rather than of the violent dying (Raphael & Martinek, 1997).

Table 1 provides a chart of different traumatic reactions and grief reactions that may occur simultaneously. The alignment of these reactions allows one to see how the traumatic reaction and grief intensify when they occur together. The following description uses metaphors to illustrate a young girl's experience of the combination of the trauma and grief reactions. This example only focuses on reactions and it does not incorporate the youth's capacities and environmental resources, which can mitigate these responses.

After The Violent Death of Her Mother ...

With avoidance and denial present, a brick wall slams down around her and all associations with the death and loss are avoided. This 14-year-old girl, whose mother was murdered by her mother's boyfriend, actively avoids all reminders about the violent death. However, she is not able to remain isolated from the reality. Behind the brick wall she is having horrific images of the death of her mother. The intrusive thoughts and images of her dead mother's body and the blood contributes further to feelings of shock and being dazed. Feeling different, she loses interest in activities she once enjoyed, shows little emotion, and feels very separate from others. This distance and lack of interest magnifies the feelings of sadness, despair, fatigue, loneliness, abandonment, guilt, and longing for her mother. Even with all of these feelings weighing her down, she remains keyed up and "on alert" for potential danger, constantly scanning her environment for violence and threats. She waits and worries about who will die next. She cannot sleep at night and in fact, she does not want to go to sleep for fear of having nightmares about her mother being stabbed to death. All of this arousal in conjunction with feeling anxious, insecure, and vulnerable without her mother has drastically intensified her anxiety. With this escalating anxiety, she reports that her brain sometimes "blacks out." With not always being able to control her mind—death images one minute, blank screen the next—she finds it increasingly difficult, actually impossible, to concentrate in school, and her grades begin to plummet.

Without full control of her mind and continuing to feel disorganized and confused in her everyday life, she begins to feel incompetent. Because she is 14 years old, some expect her to be "a responsible young adult," but the truth is that while she was starting to be more independent, her mother was the one who really helped her make good decisions. Without her mother, feelings of helplessness often overcome her, making it difficult to participate in the decision-making process. Instead, her life proceeds without a rudder to guide her—she floats but does not steer.

As she breaks though the brick wall that has been around her since the death, she slowly begins to engage in daily activities, such as school during the week and movies with friends on the weekend, but sometimes she has feelings that the death is occurring all over again. The feelings, thoughts, sights, smells, and sounds are real, happening over and over. In the midst of mundane activities like watching TV or eating dinner, cues about the violent death send her back to the night of the stabbing. With these constant traumatic experiences and profound feelings of longing, her vision of her future is blurred. She stops trying to look ahead and stays focused on only 1 minute at a time. Once again she tries to push all of the reminders about the death away but they continue to own her. She feels helpless and agitated.

When she thinks about her life without her mother, anger surges. When she thinks about how her mother died, heat rushes through her body as if a water pump has pushed scalding water through her veins. If only she could have a peaceful dream where her mother returns and tells her that she is okay and that throughout her life she will watch over her, guide and protect her. The young girl longs for a comforting dream about her mother but instead most of her dreams are about the night she "should have ... could have" stopped it from happening.

Table 1 Trauma and Grief

Grief and traumatic reactions may be occurring simultaneously or independently. One reaction may take precedence over the other and/or may be occurring more frequently or intensely. This chart aligns traumatic reactions and emotional grief reactions that may interfere with each other when occurring simultaneously. When the reactions opposite each other occur at the same time, the traumatic and grief reactions may intensify. Note that cognitive, behavioral, and physiological reactions, which are not listed, may also be occurring as well.

*Traumatic Reactions	*Emotional Grief Reactions
Reexperiencing: reoccurring recollection about the violent death	Shock, denial, daze
Avoidance: trying to stop thinking about the violent death	
Avoidance or numbing of feelings or emotions	
Loss of interest in significant activities, feeling detached from others, constricted affect	Sadness, despair, fatigue, loneliness, abandonment, guilt, longing
Hypervigilance, difficulty falling or staying asleep, physiological responses	Anxiety, fear, panic, vulnerability, insecurity
Inability to recall parts of the event, difficulty concentrating	Disorganization, confusion
Feeling like one is reliving the event, intense distress when exposed to "triggers," lack of future orientation	Helplessness
Irritability, angry outbursts, revenge fantasies	Anger
Nightmares and night terrors	Dreams about the person

*Assess intensity, frequency, and duration. Cognitive, behavioral, and physiological responses also need to be considered.

Addressing Grief and Trauma

If traumatic reactions are impinging on the bereavement process, the current clinical consensus is that trauma distress needs to be decreased first to allow the bereavement process to proceed (Cohen, et al., 2002; Nader, 1997; Pynoos & Nader, 1988). Reactions resulting from the traumatic death, such as distressing intrusive images, physiological reactions, numbing, avoidance, constricted affect, revenge, and reunion fantasies must be addressed (Pynoos & Nader, 1990; Clark, Pynoos, & Goebel, 1996). Also, it is important that coping skills are enhanced to help the adolescent manage and decrease the traumatic reactions (see chapter 9 for a discussion about coping strategies). Furthermore, bereaved adolescents who have had someone close die violently need to be helped to recall positive images of the deceased and to address the sadness of the loss (Clark, Pynoos, & Goebel, 1996) without the intrusion of trauma symptoms prohibiting or inhibiting this process. Memories about the deceased should not be overshadowed by the violent death.

Some adolescents may vacillate between traumatic distress and separation distress and the combination. Whereas decreasing traumatic distress may be the initial goal of treatment, Nader (1997) underscores the importance of following the "adolescent's own rhythm" (p. 39). Facilitators need to be in tune with individual group members' rhythm and the rhythm of the group as a whole in terms of addressing content and reactions related to the death (trauma) and the loss (grief). For example, it may be that in the initial session when members are asked to "name the person(s) who died and include the nature of the relationship of the person who died," such recollections may lead to thinking about the violent death, which then triggers traumatic reactions such as avoidance or reexperiencing. However, some adolescents may immediately be able to use the memories of the deceased's life to help counterbalance traumatic reactions.

Talking about the violent death and the surrounding factors and sharing this with other group members often helps reduce traumatic responses, such as avoidance and reexperiencing. The group sessions, including the initial screening, provide several opportunities for group members to explore the traumatic death and create a coherent narrative about what happened. Such narrative accounts may be gruesome. If young adolescents are in the group, facilitators may want to monitor the amount of detail shared by members so that others are not retraumatized and/or fixated on the horrific details. Other approaches to exploration such as drawing and writing may be utilized as a means of expression. However, if there is a sense of safety within the group environment and enhanced coping skills, adolescents in the group should be able to listen to and witness each other's experience. Older adolescents may not be as fascinated as the younger adolescents with the gory details and they also may have more coping skills allowing them to listen to each other while remaining separate from or not overwhelmed by the other members' stories. If group members begin to become overwhelmed by listening to another member talk about the violent death, they should be encouraged to utilize relaxation techniques and coping strategies that provide comfort. Session 5 provides specific activities geared toward addressing traumatic reactions.

A Word About Adult Traumatic Grief

Researchers and practitioners are in the beginning stages of understanding the complex phenomena of childhood traumatic grief. It is anticipated that the definition and criteria will evolve as we continue to learn more about traumatic grief in children and adolescents. Similarly, the concept of traumatic grief in adults is also being explored and defined (Horowitz, Siegel, Holen, Bonanno, Milbrath, & Stinson, 1997; Jacobs, Mazure, & Prigerson, 2000). Because of developmental differences, childhood traumatic grief (for children and adolescents) and adult traumatic grief are defined somewhat differently. For more information about adult traumatic grief, often referred to as complicated grief, see http://www.med.yale.edu/psych/cgrief/ or Managing Grief After Disaster: A National Center for PTSD Fact Sheet by Katherine Shear http://www.ncptsd.org/facts/disaster/fs_grief_disasterhtml.

Witnessing Violence and Violent Death

Since the 1980s, researchers have been documenting the prevalence of community violence and the high levels of violence exposure that children and adolescents experience, especially in inner cities. Studies documenting the percentages of children and youth who have witnessed homicides and suicides range from 3% to 43%. For example, in a study with 96 inner-city low-income adolescents (14- to 18-year-olds), 43% of the youth reported that they had witnessed a murder (Berman, Kurtines, Silverman, & Serafini, 1996). Fitzpatrick and Boldizar (1993) also found that 43% of their sample (221 African-American children age 6 to 18) had witnessed a murder. In another study with 1,000 urban elementary and secondary school students, more than 1 in 4 had witnessed a murder, nearly 40% had seen a shooting, and more than one third had seen a stabbing (Garbarino, Dubrow, Kostenly, & Pardo, 1992). When 37 low-income inner-city fifth and sixth graders were asked about their exposure to violence, 23% reporting seeing a dead body, 9% witnessing a murder, and 3% witnessing a suicide (Richters & Martinez, 1993). Similarly, with a sample of 99 low-income children (age 8 to 12) who lived in a high crime area, 17% reported that they had seen someone killed, 11% reported that they had seen someone commit suicide, and 10% had seen a dead body (not at a funeral) (Kliewer, Lepore, Oskin, & Johnson, 1998).

Witnessing violent death does not always occur in isolation; many children and youth are exposed to other forms of violence such as stabbings, shootings, burglary, rape, and neglected environments. For example, in a study in which 83% of low-income inner-city African-American children and adolescents reported that they knew someone who had been killed, 50% reported multiple instances of witnessing arrests and assaults and knowing people who had been shot or murdered and 30% reported knowing three or more people who had been robbed or stabbed (Overstreet, Dempsey, Graham, & Moely, 1999). The pervasiveness of violence and associated stressors such as poverty, lack of economic opportunity, dilapidated buildings, and inadequate schools may contribute significantly to youths' stress level. When working with youth who live in violent environments, group facilitators need to be cognizant of the fact that symptoms of traumatic stress may not be directly linked to the most obvious or identifiable stressor. Indeed, responses may be because of experiencing multiple stressors, which have occurred in the youths' environment over time (Spencer, Dupree, Cunningham, Harpalani, & Muñoz-Miller, 2003). Although the 10-week group format is designed to address the stress resulting from the violent death, the youth's prior and present exposure to violence and other stressors needs to be taken into account. Also, facilitators need to be aware of the youth's environmental context and intervene when possible and appropriate (as discussed in chapter 10).

When Violence Does Not Stop

When adolescents live in neighborhoods where violent crime rates (murder, assault, rape) are high, the fear of a person close to them dying of violence or being hurt is reasonable. When adolescents live in homes where domestic violence occurs, the threat of another person dying or being hurt is pervasive. Both fear and the threat of violence can significantly impact the bereavement process and the adolescent's development. Furthermore, it is difficult to decrease traumatic symptoms when the fear and threat of violence continues. In fact, the traumatic symptoms often become exaggerated and the grief delayed.

Lenore Terr (1991), an expert in childhood trauma, categorized trauma into two types. Type I occurs when a single traumatic event happens and Type II involves multiple or long-lasting traumatic occurrences. There are four common reactions that occur when a child experiences either Type I or Type II trauma: intrusive images or perceptions of the traumatic event; behavioral reenactments that repeat some aspect of the traumatic event; specific fears; and changes in attitudes about people, life, and the future. In addition to these reactions, when Type I trauma occurs, the child or youth often remembers the full details of the trauma, develops omens (assigning reasons for why the trauma happened), and has misperceptions. When Type II trauma occurs, the child or adolescent may experience the four identified reactions plus massive denial and numbing, self-hypnosis, dissociation, and rage. When an adolescent witnesses the violent death of someone close and then has to endure the trauma and loss reminders over time, both Type I and II trauma may occur. Also, adolescents who experience Type I and II trauma may use different strategies (often self destructive) to numb the pain. If the trauma distress is not resolved, character changes may occur (Terr, 1991).

Some may think that children and adolescents who live amid chronic violence "get used to it." This is wrong. "It does not appear that children traumatized by repeated sights of human aggression become immune or resistant to violence, though they may develop a variety of defenses to lessen the impact of the terror" (Eth & Pynoos, 1994, pp. 296–297). For example, as a way to deal with chronic violence, fear, and loss, children and adolescents may "act tough," act uncaring, or become aggressive or withdrawn (Osofsky, Wewers, Hann, & Fick, 1993). Children and adolescents living amid chronic violence may have to adapt in ways that others may consider dysfunctional. Whereas certain coping strategies may assist children and adolescents who continue to live in danger, their approaches may not be adaptive in other situations such as in the school environment. Furthermore, the coping strategies used during one developmental phase may not serve them well as they mature. However, Garbarino and associates (1991) recognize that many children and adolescents living in danger are resilient especially when parents are able to buffer them against the continuous stress. These authors suggest that when parents are pushed beyond their coping capacity and not able to protect their children, the child's resilient capacity may also weaken (Garbarino, Kostelny, & Dubrow, 1991).

Parent-Parent Violent Death

Some youth have had both parents die due to violence. Whether the deaths occurred from a homicide-suicide, terrorist attack, car accident or some other type of accident such as a plane crash, having both parents die can leave the adolescent devastated. When an adolescent loses both parents, he or she needs a tremendous amount of support. The bereaved youth is faced with multiple losses including the different types of support provided and roles that each parent played in the youth's development. Although other family members may not completely assume these roles in the youth's life, it is important that the adults become active in trying to offer support and guidance.

When one parent kills another parent, a multitude of challenges can arise for the youth. It is frequently the case that when one parent kills another parent, the youth has been exposed to previous domestic violence. Similar to witnessing violent death, witnessing domestic violence, especially when it has been chronic, can cause serious problems for the adolescent. For example, Frantuzzo and Mohr (1999) reported that children and adolescents exposed to domestic violence are at risk for experiencing various problems including, but not limited to, conduct problems, aggressive behavior, difficulty concentrating, poor academic and intellectual functioning, depression, low self-esteem, and anxiety. Also, when children grow up in homes in which domestic violence occurs they are at risk for experiencing other types of violence such as physical and sexual abuse.

In an attempt to understand the psychological trauma that occurs after witnessing intimate partner homicide, Pynoos and Eth (1984, 1994) interviewed children and adolescents who witnessed the homicide of a parent. Pynoos and Eth found that adolescents who witnessed the murder of a parent exhibited similar posttraumatic stress reactions as adults experienced after a traumatic event. These researchers found that adolescents after violent death were at risk for abrupt significant life changes where the youth entered adulthood earlier than they would have had the death not occurred. For example, they may drop out of school, leave home, or get married. Also, adolescents may become rebellious and engage in risky behaviors such as substance use, truancy, and situations that reenact aspects of the violence. Eth and Pynoos (1994) warn that such posttraumatic behaviors coupled with poor impulse control and reenactment behavior can lead to life-threatening situations.

Cognitively mature adolescents may be able to anticipate how the death(s) will affect their future. However, some adolescents may not even anticipate that they will have a future, perhaps because they believe their fate is similar to the deceased. Adolescents may analyze the circumstances of the violent death paying careful attention to the roles of others contributing to the death and their own actions during the dying. Harsh judgments about their own actions or inactions may lead to intense feelings of guilt (Eth & Pynoos, 1994). Intense feelings of guilt for not saving the deceased also may lead to survivor's guilt, which is feeling guilty for surviving while the other person died. With guilt often comes a host of questions and thoughts such as, "Why couldn't I have stopped it from happening?"; "Why didn't I die?"; and "If only I would have done . . . it would not have happened." Guilt can exacerbate traumatic reactions and bereavement. Although it is helpful for group facilitators and group members to tell adolescents who feel guilty that the death is not their fault, they may need to explore, question, and challenge their own reasoning (cognitive thinking) until it is clear that it is not their fault.

What Is the "Story" and Whose Is It?

Because violent death is a public matter that devastates private lives, family members and other loved ones often become entangled with many other people, officials, and systems. Indeed, "during the phases of coping with violence, families and children continue to be immersed in a web of relationships with others in their communities. Clergy, police, teachers, extended family members,

Revenge

It is not uncommon for survivors to have thoughts and feelings of revenge. These retaliatory fantasies may be complicated by peer pressure, feelings of obligation and honor, guilt, easy access to weapons, no apprehended perpetrator, and distrust and/or failure of the justice system (Temple, 1997). In today's world with guns easily accessible to youth, threats and plans about retaliation must be taken seriously. Session 7 in the group model includes a discussion about retaliation. Such a discussion among peers in a safe environment allows the youth to address their fantasies and at the same time receive feedback from peers about the possible consequences of carrying out such an act.

If the group facilitator is concerned about an adolescent having homicidal ideation, it may be helpful to have a family session in which such thoughts of retaliation can be normalized but in which supportive adults send clear messages that they do not want the adolescent to threaten or harm another person in retaliation (Salloum, 2002). Some youth, and adults, may view retaliation as justifiable, especially if the criminal justice system failed to hold someone accountable. However, the potential consequences of any family member taking retaliatory actions need to be openly discussed without minimizing the risks. If group facilitators are concerned about retaliation, they should seek supervision to discuss the homicidal risk and assessment and, if necessary, refer the adolescent to another professional who is equipped to conduct an assessment.

Facilitators need to be aware of state laws regarding "duty to warn" threatened individuals. Although such threats of retaliation should not be taken lightly, facilitators want to make sure that they are adequately assessing the threat and are prepared to intervene when adolescents are at high risk for retaliation. Hardwick and Rowton-Lee (1996) provide a framework for assessing the risk of adolescent homicide. Clinical judgment must be used when considering the salience of the presence and combination of these factors. The authors list the following factors as risks: vulnerability/background factors, which include family variables such as abuse, neglect or rejection, violence, criminality, and alcoholism; biological factors, which include brain damage, learning difficulties, impaired language, and impulsivity and attention deficit; personality and cognitive factors, which include history of aggression, problems with anger, homicidal threats and fantasies, capacity to dehumanize, morbid identity, and paranoid ideation; situational factors, which include losses, rejection in relationships, threats to manhood or self-esteem, hopelessness and helplessness, drugs/alcohol, crime, group influence, and psychiatric state. During the assessment, other factors, such as the specificity of the threats and intended victim, degree of cooperation with the clinician assessing the threat, and the degree of motivation, need to be taken into account. It is also important to assess supportive people in the youth's life who can dissuade the adolescent (Hardwick & Rowton-Lee, 1996).

Surviving After Violent Death

Coping Strategies

A main focus of the 10-week grief and trauma group model is to help adolescents cope with violent death and loss in a healthy, nondestructive manner. Coping strategies are discussed in sessions 4 through 9. The literature about coping provides some understanding about ways to help adolescents, but the research remains limited in terms of which coping strategies are most helpful for which populations after which types of violent deaths. Perhaps the simple response to these questions is that the most helpful coping strategies are ones that help the youth manage their life day by day after the death. It is important that these coping strategies are not destructive and that they promote healthy development.

Coping is defined as "constantly changing and behavioral efforts to manage specific external and/or internal demands that are appraised as taxing or exceeding the resources of the person" (Lazarus & Folkman, 1984, p. 114). This definition of coping implies that it is an ever-changing, process-oriented effort and occurs as an attempt to manage stressors. A multitude of coping approaches may be employed as the demands, appraisals, and relationships between the youth and the environment change.

Generally, there are two main categories that describe the way people cope with stress: problem-focused coping and emotion-focused coping. Problem-focused coping consists of managing, reconceptualizing, minimizing, or removing the problem causing the stress whether this involves the self and/or the environment. Emotion-focused coping consists of actions or thoughts directed toward regulating emotional responses to the problem (Lazarus & Folkman, 1984). Generally, because of adolescents' increased cognitive development, they are able to use more emotion- and problem-focused coping strategies than children (Eisenberg, Fabes, & Guthrie, 1997). Coping strategies need to be flexible and address changing situations. What may be helpful in one situation may not be useful in another. For example, although emotion-focused responses may be helpful initially after extreme stress, it may become a habitual response to dealing with stress and present long-range problems, as the coping style may not be the most effective response for future stress (van der Kolk, 1998).

Group facilitators need to encourage group members to utilize various coping strategies. For example, some youth may cope with their angry or sad feelings by watching television or going outside away from everyone (a problem-solving approach). However, in the school environment this type of response is not allowed. Therefore, youth need to be encouraged to be able to utilize other approaches to coping with these feelings (such as relaxation, deep breathing, and self-talk, which are emotion-focused strategies), so that they can use different approaches in different situations. Group members are encouraged in session 4 to identify numerous coping strategies and discuss the positive and negative benefits. It is important to acknowledge that when one strategy is used in excess without accommodating the demands of the environment and future situations, the strategy may no longer serve the adolescent well.

Recognizing that there are many events that children and adolescents cannot control, such as the death of someone close or living in high crime areas where violence is witnessed, Nolen-Hoeksema (1992) describes three types of coping strategies for children and adolescents to employ with uncontrollable stressors: reconstructing the event cognitively and/or behaviorally in a more positive way; using positive imagery and distraction; and developing reasonable proximal goals. Helping adolescents to develop a coherent narrative of the violent death, explore the meaning of the loss for them in their lives, and correct cognitive distortions and misinformation are approaches to cognitively reconstructing the death. Also, when adolescents engage in preventative actions such as joining Students Against Drunk Driving (SADD) or when youth decide to try to excel in academics as an honor to the deceased, they are behaviorally reconstructing the death in their life. Positive imagery, such as having an image and sense of a safe place or being able to utilize relaxation exercises and meditations (see sessions 4 and 5), are excellent strategies for coping with traumatic and bereavement stress. Distraction, as discussed earlier, can be helpful as well. Physical activity (sports, exercise) is a distraction activity that can provide additional health and mental health benefits. Finally, in terms of developing reasonable proximal goals, adolescents need a sense of future goals. However, because the attainment of these goals often cannot be reached until some later time in the youth's life (such as graduation from college or starting one's own business) concrete, short-term attainable goals need to be set so that the young person can experience immediate control, mastery, and success, which can motivate them to reach their future goals.

Positive Outcomes

Adolescents can be extremely resilient. Somehow, despite the stress endured because of the loss of someone close, some adolescents grow from the experience with increased maturity and a stronger sense of self and are well adjusted (Balk, 1983, 1990). The phenomenon of experiencing positive outcomes from tragic, traumatic situations is not new. However, as researchers began exploring the effects of trauma, they started to document the growth that occurred from experiencing trauma (known as posttraumatic growth). Bereaved people, whether traumatized or not, also have reported positive personal experiences as a result of the death.

Studies have documented some of the positive outcomes that adolescents have reported after a death. For example, Oljtenbruns (1991) found that 96% of adolescents (ranging in age from 16 to 22) identified at least one positive outcome as a result of their grief experience. More than 50% reported that because of their experience they had a deeper appreciation of life, showed greater caring for loved ones, strengthened emotional bonds with others, and felt that they had developed emotional strength. Other benefits were increased empathy, better communication skills, enhanced problem-solving skills, understanding death as part of life, increased awareness, less fear about death, increased understanding of others' reactions to death, a change in priorities, more independence, and exploration religion. In another study of 53 adolescents who had experienced the death of a friend, mostly from a violent death, 38% reported that they had become closer to friends, 34% reported that they felt they could share their feelings more freely, and 34% indicated their behavior changed such that they take time to tell people they care about them. Other positive changes included wearing seat belts, spending more time with family, becoming closer with family, joining SADD, and decreasing alcohol consumption (Schachter, 1991).

In the immediate aftermath of violent death, positive outcomes may not have occurred yet or be visible. However, after future experiences and reflection, positive outcomes may become present with some adolescents. If adolescent group members, who may vary in terms of the time since the death, are able to share some of the growth that they have experienced, it may provide hope for other group members. In the last session when group members are reflecting upon their experience in the group, facilitators may inquire about positive outcomes. Below is a list of positive outcomes that bereaved adolescents have reported.

Some Positive Outcomes . . .

More mature	Share feelings more freely
Tell and show people that they care about them	Feel closer to family
Take safety precautions and not engage in risky behaviors	Spend more time with family
Became an activist	More spiritual
Closer to friends	Stronger emotionally
Deeper appreciation of life	Better communication skills
Know self better	More empathy
Enhanced problem-solving skills	
Better understanding of death as part of life	Less fear about death
Aware of own priorities in life	More independent
Increased awareness of self, others, and the world	Deep appreciation of religion

---

Maintaining a Connection

Maintaining a connection to the deceased is a coping strategy that can be very helpful for bereaved adolescents. Earlier theories of bereavement suggested that having an ongoing relationship with the deceased was pathological and that the bereaved needed to "let go" and forget. However, when a loved one dies, forgetting may not be possible or healthy. In fact, " . . . it may be normative for mourners to maintain a presence and connection with the deceased and that this presence is not static" (Silverman, Nickman, & Worden, 1992, p. 494). Also, seeing, hearing, smelling, and even touching the deceased should not be automatically viewed as pathological. Such occurrences seem to be quite common among the bereaved. Also, those who have not had such experiences may long for them (Balk, 1983).

Research (Silverman, Nickman, & Worden, 1992) suggests that some children and adolescents who have had a parent die maintain a connection with the deceased. To date, most of this research has been with children and adolescents who have had a parent or sibling die. Having an ongoing connection with the deceased is seen as a conscious cognitive process that changes over time. Such a dynamic internal connection and representation provides a process for helping children and adolescents cope with the loss, realize the reality of the loss, and explore the meaning of the loss in their life. Moreover, maintaining a positive psychological connection with the deceased can serve as a protective factor (Black, 1984).

Silverman, Nickman, and Worden (1992) propose five categories that indicate efforts to maintain a connection with the deceased: (1) locating the deceased, (2) having experiences with the deceased in some way, (3) initiating some type of connection, (4) remembering, and (5) retaining a possession of the deceased. From these authors' research with 125 parentally bereaved children, efforts to maintain a connection were evident by most (70%) indicating that they believed the deceased was in heaven and/or had a soul with living qualities (see, hear, and move) and that their parent was watching over them (81%). Furthermore, 57% of these children reported that even 4 months after the death they spoke to their deceased parent and 90% reported that they think about their deceased parent several times a week. In addition, 77% indicated that they had a personal belonging of the deceased. In another interesting study about ongoing connections, Hogan and DeSantis (1992) asked 144 adolescents (age 13 to 18, time since death ranged from 3 months to 5 years) who had a sibling die, "If you could ask or tell your dead sibling something, what would it be?" Notions of anticipating when they would be together again, seeking guidance from the deceased, never forgetting them, searching for reasons for the death, talking with the deceased about the present time, and sharing regrets were all common themes. These findings suggest that many siblings continued to remain connected, emotionally and socially, with their deceased sibling (Hogan & DeSantis, 1992).

This notion of maintaining connections challenges the belief that a main task of grieving is "letting go" or disengaging from the deceased. With this in mind, words such as accommodation, instead of closure or recovery, may be more suitable when discussing bereavement. Accommodation implies an ever-changing negotiation of the meaning of the loss (Silverman, Nickman, & Worden, 1992). When conducting group work with adolescents after violent death, group facilitators should educate the members about the phenomenon of ongoing connections. Such education can be useful for youth who have had experiences of contact with the deceased and/or who want to know how to continue to feel connected. Facilitators also need to explore if such connections comfort them or make them feel scared. Furthermore, it needs to be clear that not everyone has these experiences so that youth who do not maintain a connection do not feel different, sad or guilty. It may be that such connections do not occur as intensely or as long when the survivor was not emotionally close to the deceased. Also, facilitators need to be aware if the religious affiliations or cultural identity of group members encourage or discourage such connections (a worksheet about maintaining connections is provided in session 6).

Consider the Context

Although one of the main goals of the time-limited group is to decrease posttraumatic symptoms associated with the violent death, facilitators may need to address other areas and issues to enhance the bereaved adolescents' adjustment. As Bard, Arnone, and Nemiroff (1986) state, "It is our [*facilitators*] obligation to come to understand the nature of the environmental contexts in which people try to come to terms with trauma" (p. 303, italics added). Therefore, facilitators need to ask, "How does the context affect the bereaved adolescent's ability to cope with the violent death and loss?"

The time-limited grief and trauma group intervention must be used in conjunction with the ecological perspective. Brofenbrenner's (1989) ecological framework suggests that people must be viewed in the context of their environment and that bidirectional processes occur within and between various systems. Therefore, the bereaved adolescent after violent death is influenced and influences dynamic interactions that occur within and between various systems. These interactions continuously change over time, affecting the youth's development. Figure 10.1, "Ecological perspective with adolescents after violent death," illustrates the five different systems: microsystem, mesosystem, exosystem, macrosystem, and chronosystem.

As Figure 10.1 indicates, there are many death-related factors associated with the violent death that may add additional stress for the adolescent. Factors associated with the violent death include: witnessing the violent death and/or aftermath; the presence of physically wounded survivors; level of violence and/or threat prior to the event, during the event, and after the event; closeness of the relationship; whether the event was mass violence or a single incident; funeral experiences; whether the body is absent or disfigured; and experiences with the criminal justice process. Any and all of these factors have the potential for causing extreme stress, overwhelming the adolescent's coping capacity. Many of these factors can cause ongoing challenges. However, with the adolescent's personal resources and strengths, and resources and strengths from environmental systems, the adolescent may be better equipped to manage the stress and make successful adjustments.

The adolescent's developmental status, including coping abilities, and perception of the violent death may affect how he or she interacts with others in his or her immediate environment (the macrosystem), which in turn will affect the youth's development. (See chapter 3 for a discussion about adolescence and adolescent bereavement.) However, other people's experience of the violent

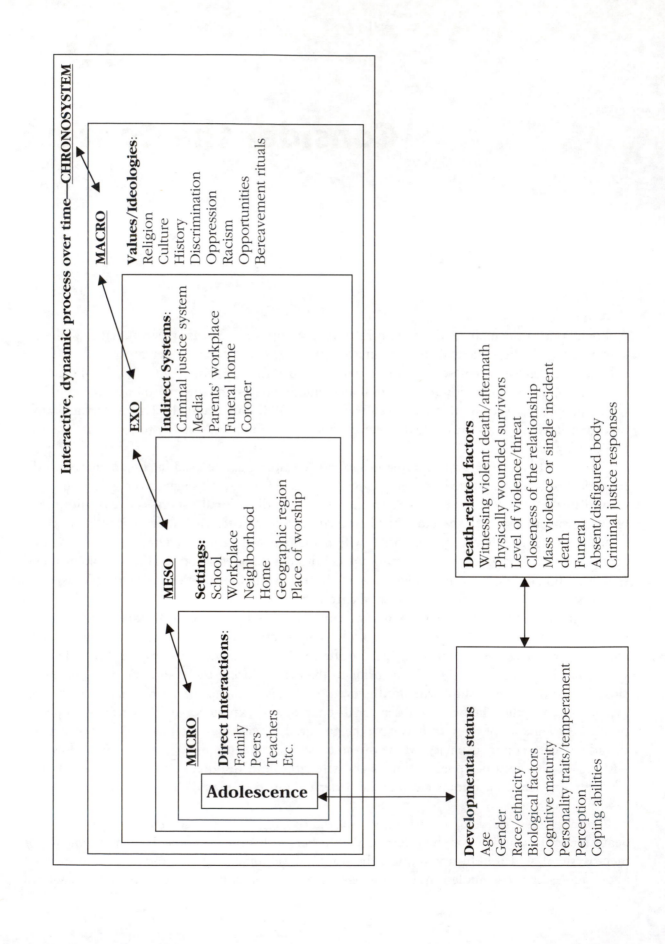

death may dictate how they communicate with the youth and their interactions in turn may affect the youth's response. This bidirectional process is most commonly seen with adolescents and their parents. For example, the youth's perception of the violent death and coping may depend on the parent's beliefs and views about the violent death and on the parent's ability to support the adolescent and buffer him or her from ongoing stress. Also, as discussed in chapter 3, a parent may rely on an adolescent to take on more responsibility, especially if the other parent died. This assumed role of the adolescent may help the surviving parent cope better, which in turn allows the parent to emotionally support the youth and deal with ongoing challenges. However, for some adolescents the new role may cause additional stress, creating tension in interactions with the parent, which in turn can cause more stress for the adolescent and parent. Session 8 in the group model encourages adolescent group members to identify how family members and interactions have changed since the violent death.

The microsystem represents all the direct interactions and activities in the youth's face-to-face settings (Bronfenbrenner, 1989). These exchanges are between the people the adolescent interacts with, such as parents, extended family, peers, and teachers. Because these people may be affected by the violent death and their interactions affect the adolescent, facilitators may consider providing some intervention with others in the microsystem. For example, as discussed in chapters 11 and 12, facilitators can conduct group meetings with parents and teachers to provide education about the effects of violence and death on adolescents and about ways to support bereaved youth. Also, teachers may need to be provided with information about ways to help peers be supportive of bereaved adolescents. Furthermore, adolescents are often concerned about the well-being of their bereaved siblings and referrals for intervention services may need to be made to assist siblings or other close family members.

The mesosystem involves the different settings that the youth engages in and the linkages that take place between two or more settings (such as school and home, home and neighborhood, and school and workplace) (Bronfenbrenner, 1989). Interactions occurring in the mesosystem can significantly influence the functioning of the youth. Facilitators need to be cognizant of the linkages between systems that may affect the youth's coping. When one system is supportive and another is not, such as family and school, this may cause conflict for the adolescent. As discussed in the microsystem, facilitators may need to intervene between systems, such as by encouraging teacher-parent meetings.

The exosystem involves the processes that take place between two or more settings, which indirectly influences the youth even though the youth only has contact with one system (Bronfenbrenner, 1989). An example of this is the relationship between the parent and the parent's workplace. For example, if the parent's employer does not allow the parent time off to attend the trial, this may cause additional stress for the parent, which in turn may affect the interactions between the youth and his or her parent. Another example of interactive systems in the exosystem that may affect bereaved youth would be the relationship between the youth's school and the community mental health center. For example, these two systems—school and mental health center—could arrange for therapeutic services such as a time-limited grief and trauma group to be held at school for bereaved youth in need.

The macrosystem consists of overarching patterns, such as values, laws, culture, subculture, beliefs, characteristics, attitudes, opportunities, resources, and hazards, which are within all of the systems (Bronfenbrenner, 1989). The youth and his or her family may ascribe to or be affected by certain patterns, while others with whom they interact within their environment may be affected differently. For example, the general cultural belief in the youth's environment may be that the bereaved should not grieve in public or after the burial, but the youth's culture may encourage public expression. These differences may cause conflict or support for the adolescent, depending upon their interactions and development. Resources and opportunities can help lessen the stress for adolescents and their families. However, when environments are not supportive, such as deficient schools and lack of economic opportunity, the adolescent and family may experience additional stress.

The chronosystem recognizes that the adolescent and environment and all of the interactive processes are interconnected and change over time (Bronfenbrenner, 1989). Although the time-limited group only lasts 10 weeks, facilitators need to be aware that changes may be occurring within the youth and within other systems during this short time frame. Also, facilitators need to provide both the youth and their family with information about community resources should assistance be needed in the future.

Facilitators may not be able to intervene in all of the systems but they need to be aware of how the systems and interactions affect the youth. Also, it is helpful for facilitators to be linked with other groups such as advocacy groups and policy makers who can intervene within systems.

Following are some examples of ways that facilitators can involve other systems to benefit the bereaved youth:

- Link the youth with a tutor to assist with academics.
- Link the youth with a mentor, which may help with identity issues.
- Educate classmates about grief and ways to respond appropriately to grieving peers.
- Conduct a family session to facilitate communication about the death and loss.
- Arrange meetings between homicide detectives and family members.
- Educate prosecutors who have children and adolescents as witnesses.
- Offer services to siblings to lessen the burden of the adolescent sibling who may be placed in the role of caretaker.
- Educate teachers about grief and trauma and ways to assist the adolescent.
- Inform adolescents of community events that promote connection with their neighborhood.
- Provide case management services to families who may have housing and financial needs because of the death.
- Invite youth to violence prevention workshops or other educational events.
- Educate local officials about the need for mental health services after violent death.
- Work with policy makers to create safer environments for youth and to provide accessible and affordable mental health services for all youth.
- Get involved with organizations that strive to create safe environments for children, adolescents, and families.

Ethnic/Racial and Cultural Influences

McGoldrick et al. (1991) suggest that before working with a specific population, the following questions about the particular cultural traditions of the group need to be explored:

1. What are the prescribed rituals for handling dying, the dead body, the disposal of the body, and rituals to commemorate the loss?
2. What are the group's beliefs about what happens after death?
3. What do they believe about appropriate emotional expression and integration of a loss experience?
4. What are the gender rules for handling the death?
5. Are certain deaths particularly stigmatized (e.g., suicide) or traumatic for the group (e.g., the death of a child in Puerto Rican culture)? (p. 179)[1]

"Each cultural group provides the means for its members to channel their grief though specific rituals to complete the common tasks and issues of bereavement" (Kagawa-Singer, 1998, p. 1751). Therefore, facilitators need to be familiar with the cultural practices of different groups in terms of death and bereavement. If facilitators are not aware of and understand the grief responses and rituals of the group they are working with, they may come to inappropriate conclusions (Oltjenbruns, 1998), and in fact may not be helpful to the bereaved. Grief and trauma groups need to incorporate culturally sensitive approaches (Schilling, Koh, Abramovitz, & Gilbert, 1992).

Whether cultural differences are based on race/ethnicity, religion, or geographic region, facilitators are encouraged to think about how the time-limited grief and trauma group may be modified to meet the needs of group members. Facilitators and group members need to be sensitive to different cultural mourning processes. Therefore, facilitators need to be educated about the cultural practices that affect the group members after violent death. (See Appendix B for additional resources regarding culture, bereavement, and trauma.)

The next two sections provide some information about the bereavement cultural practices of two groups: African Americans and Latinos. The two groups were chosen because they represent the largest ethnic minority groups in the United States and because information regarding the bereavement cultural practices within these two groups is limited. Information about these populations should be used with great caution, as these groups are extremely heterogeneous. The information cannot be generalized, because there is a wide range of differences within groups: Every person has a unique experience. However, the information in the two sections highlights the importance of recognizing cultural differences when working with various groups such as African-American or Latino/a adolescents.

African Americans and Death

The overall death rate of African Americans is high compared to other ethnic and racial groups (Freid, Prager, MacKay, & Xia, 2003). In terms of violent death, the African-American population has been disproportionately affected by the homicide rate. For example, in 1999, blacks were six times more likely than whites to be murdered (U.S. Department of Justice, 2001), with homicide being the leading cause of death for African-American youth (ages 15 to 24; 54.7 per 100,000)

(National Vital Statistics, 2000). Death rates are often higher because of environmental factors that disproportionately affect African Americans, such as limited access to health care, poverty, racism, and chronically stressful urban environments. Therefore, an ecological perspective must be considered when working with this population. The ecological perspective must consider the youth's and family's strengths, informal and formal resources, and how other environmental factors (Johnson-Moore & Phillips, 1994) affect the adolescent's and family's response to the death and loss (for a list of strengths and resources assessment questions, see chapter 14). Due to the high death rate, facilitators will want to assess for prior losses and deaths and how this has affected the youth. If multiple losses have occurred, facilitators should allow the youth to choose which loss or losses he or she wants to address. However, facilitators need to be aware of which loss might contribute to the youth experiencing traumatic symptoms and respectfully encourage the youth to focus on that loss (see chapter 15 for more information about multiple losses).

For many African Americans, death is viewed as "God's will" (Hines, 1991, p. 187), even when the death occurred by violent means. Death also may be seen as a "necessary step to achieve a new life—free from pain, suffering, and sorrow" (Hines, 1991, p. 187). Johnson-Moore and Phillips (1994) suggest that such positive beliefs that are linked with faith are ways for many African Americans to cope with multiple losses and challenges. Religion and spirituality can help one maintain the perspective that one will survive and "that things will get better" (Johnson-Moore & Phillips (1994, p. 110). Facilitators will want to explore the adolescent's beliefs about death and the afterlife and how these beliefs help him or her cope. Furthermore, it is important that facilitators are able to provide a safe environment in which adolescents can discuss issues of spirituality and faith. Although the African-American youth's family may express beliefs that the death was "God's will" or that it was the deceased person's time to "go home," some African-American adolescents may need to explore conflicts between faith and anger toward senseless violence, and toward God. Such exploration must be conducted in a way that does not disrespect the family's beliefs but allows the youth to express inner conflicts and questions. Also, facilitators may consider linking the youth and family with churches or religious leaders in the community for sources of ongoing support (Johnson-Moore & Phillips, 1994) if the family is not already involved with a church and/or if they would find this to be helpful. However, when such linkages are made, facilitators will want to make sure those religious leaders are knowledgeable about grief, trauma, and the effects of violent death. Furthermore, facilitators may consider actually conducting the time-limited grief and trauma groups at a church in the community in which a large number of African-American adolescents have been affected by violent death. Also, it may be that an African-American youth minister or other religious member may serve as a co-facilitator, as the youths may already have established rapport and trust with this person.

Funeral Practices

As Hines (1991) explains, for many African Americans there is usually a tremendous amount of importance placed on the funeral. Children are often included in the rituals surrounding death and burial. Further, displaying grief publicly is not uncommon, especially among women and children. In fact, the eulogy, music and an open casket all may be conducted in a way that encourages an emotional release (Hines, 1991). However, there is much diversity with African-American funerals. Hines (1991) notes that, in the northeast, some African Americans conduct wakes at a church or funeral parlor on the evening preceding the funeral. In the south, some African Americans partake in the ritual of "sitting up," which "involves family and friends bringing food or money and visiting the family from the time of death until the funeral" (Hines, 1991, p. 188). Funeral customs are influenced not only by geography but also by religion, economic background, and level of community involvement. Stereotypical views—such as, Pentecostal and Southern Baptist funerals include long sermons with a lot of emotionalism—may not be the case with every Pentecostal or Southern Baptist funeral (Perry, 1993). Facilitators will want to explore the adolescent's role and experience at the funeral. Also, as food and music are often used as comfort and for expression, facilitators may want to include both of these in the group sessions.

The African-American culture values "being strong" (i.e., handling adversity without tears or diminished performance). Crying and grieving are considered appropriate and necessary for healing, especially for a few weeks after the funeral. However, as the weeks pass, even though the grieving continues, one is expected to continue with daily functioning without an ongoing display of sadness (Hines, 1991). Facilitators will want to explore how the adolescent expressed grief right after the funeral and if later that has changed. Also, if this information is relevant for the specific African American(s) in the group, facilitators need to caution against thinking that the adolescent is not grieving just because he or she is not presenting a sad demeanor.

Facilitators need to be aware of how different cultures view expression of feelings. Lee (1995) explains that many African-American inner-city children mask their feelings to help them stay in control. Many of these children are exposed to constant death and violence. Having an opportunity to communicate with others who have had similar experiences may help them to understand their reactions. Many of these reactions can be seen as normal reactions to abnormal events that have occurred in their environment. Facilitators need to safeguard against pathologizing African-American adolescents and consider their "masked" reactions as perhaps protective ones, especially when they are living in hostile environments.

Family ties, which often include contact with a large network of relatives and fictive kin, are highly valued among African Americans (Gibbs, 2001). Therefore, facilitators must not assume the significance of the nature of the relationship between the adolescent and the deceased. "One cannot make assumptions about the meaning of a death simply on the basis of immediacy of the relationship; a relationship with a member of the extended family may hold as great or greater significance for an individual than a relationship with a member of the nuclear family" (Hines, 1991, p. 191).

Some African-American adolescents may present as withdrawn and/or hostile, and may not be comfortable with self-disclosure, especially if the facilitator is white and viewed as an authority figure. It is recommended that the facilitators be active, outgoing, directive, and open when establishing rapport. In addition, the facilitators should encourage African-American adolescents to discuss their ambivalence about being in therapy, their fears about being labeled "crazy" by their peers, and their reluctance to disclose their feelings and concerns to a stranger (Gibbs, 2001).

Latinos and Death

The terms *Hispanic* and *Latino* are often used interchangeably among the majority population in the United States. In some regions of the country, the term Hispanic may be preferred, whereas in other regions Latino may be more commonly used. Similarly, one person may prefer Latino, whereas another may use Hispanic. These labels represent people in the United States from many different countries such as Mexico, Cuba, Nicaragua, Costa Rica, Brazil, Columbia, and so on.

In this section, when the more specific group, such as *Puerto Rican* or *Mexican*, is stated in the literature, it will be used; otherwise, the term Latino will be used.

Many Latinos view death as an extension of life. Children are taught early not to fear death, as it is part of life (Munet-Vilaró, 1998). Munet-Vilaró states that based on her practice experience with this population, such beliefs seem to have a positive influence in the early phases of the grief process. However, while death is seen as a part of life, when it is sudden or traumatic (especially when a child dies), it is much harder to accept (Garcia-Preto, 1991). Facilitators need to be aware of this, especially if the person who died violently was a child. Facilitators may want to inform the entire family about supportive resources. However, such services may not be accepted immediately. Not realizing that adolescents may experience psychological problems because of the death and the belief that support is to be sought from within the family and not from outsiders, that personal matters should be kept private, and that facilitators are not culturally sensitive, may become barriers for Latino families to accept services (Chachkes & Jennings, 1994), including consenting for the youth to participate in group counseling. Acculturation and support from extended family may have a significant impact on these barriers (Chachkes & Jennings, 1994). Facilitators will want to be aware of the degree of acculturation of the adolescent and the family and how this may affect the adolescent. Latino/a adolescents, whether they are immigrants or U.S.-born, may experience acculturation stress because of living between cultures, discrimination, and intergenerational acculturation gaps (Hovey & King, 1996; Romero & Roberts, 2003). Acculturated Latino/a adolescents who may not speak Spanish well may not be able to participate in reminiscing about the deceased when older family members recount stories of the person's life in Spanish. This may be particularly true if the deceased is buried in the country of origin and the adolescent, who does not speak Spanish well, attends the funeral. Also, Latino/a adolescents may be expected to participate in family obligations, which may increase as a result of the death, and this may cause additional stress for the acculturated adolescent.

Issues of acculturation may become apparent in the group. For example, if group facilitators encourage members to share a drawing or writing with their parents and a Latino/a adolescent has parents who have strong beliefs that such personal information should not be shared with "outsiders," the adolescent may be reluctant to complete the assignment. The facilitator may consider conducting a family session where the family's beliefs can be respected and the adolescent can share some of the work they have accomplished in the group sessions. Also, if that particular family speaks Spanish as their first language, it may be more comfortable for the family to talk about issues related to the death and grief in Spanish (Chachkes & Jennings, 1994). Therefore, having a Spanish-speaking facilitator may be needed when working with some Latino/a adolescents and their families. Also, if there are not other Latino adolescents in the group who have similar customs and beliefs, the Latino/a adolescent may be hesitant to share with the group members about culturally specific rituals, ceremonies, and coping strategies. Therefore, facilitators need to educate all group members about differences and promote respect.

Research

Research regarding Latinos and expression of grief is scarce (Grabowski & Frantz, 1993). The following limited information discusses some of the recent findings in the literature. As mentioned earlier, facilitators must exercise caution in using this research, as there are many individual differences within groups. However, it is important to consider how specific ethnic and cultural influences may impact the grief process and how these differences may be used to make the group activities more meaningful for the specific group members.

Grabowski and Frantz (1993) found that adult Latinos (primarily Puerto Rican, Roman Catholics) experienced significantly greater grief intensity after a sudden death than Anglo individuals. Grabowski and Frantz hypothesized that this finding may be because of Puerto Ricans' valuing being with a dying relative, completing unresolved conflicts, and freeing the deceased into the afterlife, and the failure to be able to participate in these practices intensified the grief. Facilitators need to assess if the group member witnessed the violent death. Although this may further complicate one's grieving process, in fact it may be of some comfort to a Puerto Rican person to have been there during the last moments. In addition, at some point during the group, facilitators may want to include activities that encourage members to state things they wish they could have said before the person died. For this population, it may be helpful to raise unresolved conflicts and to assist with these feelings.

Another study (Oltjenbruns, 1998) with 39 Mexican-American and 61 Anglo-American college students found significant differences between the groups, with the Mexican Americans externalizing their grief more and reporting more physiological reactions resulting from the loss than the Anglo students. Facilitators need to include a careful assessment of physical reactions that have or are occurring.

Funeral Practices

For many Latinos, both males and females are expected to express emotions intensely at the time of the death, during the viewing and at the funeral. Women, in particular, may lose control and display behavior known as "ataques" (Garcia-Preto, 1991).

A unique cultural mourning practice of Catholic Latinos includes the Novena (Grabowski & Frantz, 1993; Munet-Vilaró, 1998). The Novena is based on the teachings of the Catholic religion. Munet-Vilaró (1998) explains:

> A Novena takes place a day after the person has been buried, and, for the next nine days, a rosary is said in that person's name by friends and relatives at the home of the deceased. The house of the deceased is kept closed during the day to allow the family to mourn undisturbed. This Novena is believed to help the soul find its way to heaven with all sins forgiven. People dress in black, white, or purple, and candles are lit.
>
> Refreshments are served after each rosary, and conversations related to the qualities of the deceased are encouraged. Crying at the time is allowed if the deceased was an adult, but it is seldom encouraged if the deceased was a child. Some Latinos hold the strong belief that children who die are angels and that crying for them will wet their wings and prevent them from "flying to heaven." (p. 1762)[2]

The year following the death, it is common for family members to visit the grave and continue to pray for the deceased person's soul. Also, if unresolved issues with the deceased are present, Puerto Ricans may visit a spiritist. If the person has dreams about the deceased returning to say goodbye or delivering a special message, this is seen as a sign that the deceased's spirit is restless and needs to communicate before leaving the material world (Garcia-Preto, 1991). It is very important to know these specific cultural rituals so that they are not seen in terms of pathology.

For example, without knowing that it is common to visit the grave for a year, one may view this as the person having a difficult time with the death. Also, concern about the deceased's soul is very important and, although dreams about the person may be comforting to some, it may have a completely different meaning to some Puerto Rican adolescents. If the group has members from different ethnic groups, it is important to educate the group about differences and insist on respecting one another's different beliefs. This should be included in the initial session when group rules are being established.

Notes

1. From *Living Beyond Loss: Death in the Family,* edited by Froma Walsh and Monica McGoldrick. Copyright © 1991 by Froma Walsh and Monica McGoldrick. Used by permission of W.W. Norton & Company, Inc.

2. From *Grieving and Death Rituals of Latinos,* by F. Munet-Vilaró, 1998, *Oncology Nursing Forum, 25,* p. 1762. Reprinted with permission.

Part II

Group Work with Adults in the Adolescent's Life

Parents and Guardians

Importance of Parental Support

When a group of adolescents were asked how adults could help comfort bereaved youth and what advice they would give to adults to help youth deal with death and grief, the majority of them reported that talking and listening were the most important approaches (Morin & Welsh, 1996). Research with bereaved adolescents has identified parents as a major source of support for adolescents in coping with death (Hogan & DeSantis, 1994; Ringler & Hayden, 2000). In fact, parental support is one of the main protective factors for helping youth after violent death. However, many parents (or guardians) do not know what to say or how to help their grieving teen. Moreover, parents may not talk about what happened for fear of upsetting their adolescent child further and youth may not talk to parents for fear of being a burden to them. The result of this type of protection is often silence. Yet, both may be experiencing hurt and worrying about the other.

It is important for group facilitators to try to foster parental support of bereaved youth. Perhaps the first step is to help parents understand the impact of violence and death on their child. Education about grief and trauma is imperative. Once parents understand grief and traumatic reactions they will be better prepared to help their child cope with the aftermath. Parents also need to be informed about additional resources in the community that may be able to assist them now and in the future as they continue to cope with often long-lasting effects and adjustments. The parents' task of helping their child during this time is not easy; stress can be very high. Therefore, it is important for parents to remember and practice stress-relieving activities and to encourage other family members to do the same.

This chapter provides facilitators with a 1-hour group meeting format for parents to help them help their child. The four main components of the parent group include educating parents about adolescents' reactions after violent death, ways for parents to respond, resources for parents to help their family, and tips for promoting relaxation. It is best to conduct the parent group before the adolescent group begins so that the parents can support their child in attending the sessions. This one-time group also can be held with parents in the immediate aftermath of violent death whether their child participates in a time-limited grief and trauma group or not because it provides useful information for parents. Also, facilitators may want to use sections of this parent format with a group of parents even if a death has not occurred, as a way to educate them should a death happen that affects their child.

When a violent death impacts an entire school community or group of youth, efforts should be made to provide education to all parents. This may be accomplished by distributing letters and informational handouts, using the media and/or holding a parent meeting, such as the one presented in this manual. Parents of youth who did not know the deceased and who did not witness the violence may assume that their child is not affected. That may be true. However, research suggests that youth who knew the deceased indirectly, or who may have a friend who was close to the deceased, may exhibit symptoms of posttraumatic stress (Pfefferbaum, Seale et al., 2000). Furthermore, youth who did not witness the violent dying or know the deceased but who were exposed to a lot of media coverage may also have symptoms of posttraumatic stress (Pfefferbaum, Seale et al., 2000; Terr et al., 1997). Therefore, parents need to be educated about the potential effects on adolescents of surviving, witnessing, and hearing about violent death so that they can support and protect their children.

When parents have had someone close die violently or witnessed violent death, they too may benefit from a time-limited grief and trauma group. Although the optimal approach may be to have a parents' group occurring simultaneously with the youth group, this is not always practical, as group work frequently occurs in settings such as school and youth centers where parents are not present. However, if the group occurs at a time when parents and adolescents could attend, it would be ideal to offer a parent group. Because there are many differences between adults and adolescents, group interventions designed specifically for adults after violent death should be used (see the end of this chapter for group models for adults after violent death).

Effects of Violent Death on Parents

When parents have had someone close die violently and/or if they witnessed the violence, they, too, will experience a range of reactions. Many of the same factors that apply to youth, such as closeness of the relationship, proximity to violence, and prior functioning, affect the parents' level of distress and ability to cope. After violent death of someone close, parents, like children and adolescents, may experience grief, trauma, and traumatic grief (as discussed in chapter 7). Parents who have had a child die violently are especially at risk for posttraumatic stress since such an experience can be devastating. For example, Murphy et al. (1999) found that 40% of the mothers who had a child die due to violence (accidents, suicide, homicide) met criteria for posttraumatic stress symptoms 4 months after the death and 14% of fathers met criteria for PTSD 4 months after the death. Two years after the death of the child, 21% of the mothers and 14% of the fathers exhibited PTSD symptoms. Of note is that mothers and fathers who had a child die due to homicide, as opposed to suicide and accidents, were twice as likely to meet criteria for PTSD. Murphy and associates also found that bereaved parents with PTSD reported higher rates of depression, anxiety, hostility, intense grief, low self-esteem and self-efficacy, poor coping strategies, less acceptance of death, less social support, and reported being nonproductive at work. Furthermore, mothers with PTSD consumed twice as many alcoholic beverages than mothers without PTSD. In fact, 15% of the mothers with PTSD reported consumption of more than 20 drinks per week. In addition, fathers with PTSD reported having poorer physical health than those without PTSD.

Bereaved parents need to be encouraged to find healthy ways to address their own grief. Parents may express to mental health practitioners, "If you can help my child cope with this, I will be okay." Of course, helping the youth cope with the death and loss may in fact decrease the parents' stress level, but parents may be avoiding their own grief, which in turn may have a significant impact on the adolescent's well-being.

For facilitators working with youth whose parents have had a child die due to violent death, poor adjustment and poor health among parents after violent death has several implications. First, parents need to be educated about common reactions after violent death. Because some parents may be at risk for PTSD and other mental and physical health concerns, parent education needs to include information about posttraumatic stress and how such stress can affect other areas of one's life such as work and health. As with adolescents, parents need to be educated about the potential risk for increasing alcohol consumption and, if needed, be provided with resources for evaluation for psychotropic medication and/or substance abuse treatment. When providing education to parents, a list of resources from which parents can receive help should be provided. Hopefully, by providing such education in a caring manner, the stigma associated with experiencing mental health problems and with seeking assistance can be minimized.

Parent Group: "Reactions, Responses, Resources, and Relaxation"

The following agenda is to be used during the 1-hour educational group for parents and guardians of adolescents. Handouts are available on the following pages. Also, a blank outline is included for facilitators to write their own notes for conducting the 1-hour parent group session. Material in the previous 10 chapters provides facilitators with additional information that parents may want to know. Facilitators may need to alter the format to address unique situations. For example, when presenting to parents after a suicide of their child's classmate, more information about suicide may need to be included. If a shooting occurred on campus, school officials may need to be included in the presentation to answer questions about school safety, or if a terrorist attack impacts an entire community, more emphasis may need to be placed on resources and safety. There is a section in the group format called "specific information" that can be used to address unique concerns.

Agenda

I. Introduction (5 minutes)

If the parent group is being hosted by another organization, officials from that group (i.e., school administrators, youth counselors) should introduce the facilitator as a way to provide credibility and encourage trust. Facilitators need to provide a brief overview of the agenda. If there is a small group (20 or fewer) allow for questions throughout. However, with large groups, facilitators may ask that questions be held until the end as a way to ensure that all information is presented.

II. Reactions: Effects of Violent Death on Adolescents (15 minutes)

A. Adolescents' reactions to violent death
Discuss common adolescent bereavement reactions (see chapter 3).

B. Traumatic responses
Discuss how traumatic reactions may interfere with the grief process (see chapters 6 and 7). Let parents know that while they may have a general estimate of the distress level of their adolescents, they may underestimate the severity of posttraumatic stress symptoms due to many of the symptoms being internalized and difficult to observe. Refer parents to the handout, "Helping Adolescents: When Traumatic Reactions Interfere With Grief."

C. Signs to look for
Parents need to know what may be considered typical and when they need to be concerned and seek help for their adolescent. Highlight the signs to look for listed in the handout, "How Do I Know If My Teenager Needs Help?" Emphasize that some adolescents (and adults) may use alcohol or other substances to try to numb the pain and this will lead to more problems.

D. Specific information
Information that addresses the specific needs of the parents regarding the death may need to be discussed. For example, parents may want information about suicide, about ways to memorialize the deceased or about safety concerns. It is helpful to talk with some parents or others who are knowledgeable about the group's concerns and needs before the one-time meeting so that facilitators can tailor the information to address these issues.

III. Responding: Ways to Help Adolescents Cope (15 minutes)

A. Discuss ways that parents can help adolescents after violent death (See handout "How Can Parents Help Adolescents After Violent Death?")
Discuss the importance of talking and allowing questions, creating a sense of safety, providing information, and promoting activities to foster development and health.

B. Benefits of grief and trauma group
If the parents have adolescents who will be attending a time-limited grief and trauma group, provide an overview of the themes that will be discussed (see group outline in Chapter 16) and the potential benefits (which are listed in chapter 2). Encourage parents to talk with their child and ask their child questions about their experiences in the group sessions, such as: Is there anything you want to share with me that you did in group today? However, inform parents that they need to respect their child's response and not push them to share if they do not want to.

IV. Discussion: Questions and Answers (15 minutes)

It is important to allow time for questions and answers and comments. Parents need to be able to ask their questions. Also, facilitators can encourage other parents to respond to the questions if other parents have helpful suggestions. It is important for facilitators to manage this time so that the group ends on time. If there are still questions or concerns, facilitators need to let parents know how they can get the information they need. The resources discussed in the next section may be able to provide further assistance.

V. Resources and Relaxation (10 minutes)

Facilitators may need to provide a written list of helpful community resources. Some of the national organizations (see Appendix A) may be helpful, but often parents need to know about local services. Local information such as support groups, victims support advocacy programs (such as at the District Attorney's office), crime victims reparations information, local MADD chapters, mental health services, and financial assistance programs may be helpful.

If facilitators are conducting a grief and trauma group with adolescents, the parents need to know how they can contact the facilitators. Also, parents need to know where they can go for help for themselves. Information to help all family members affected by the violence needs to be provided. It is important to destigmatize mental health intervention, and make it clear that seeking help is not a sign of weakness but rather of strength and protection.

Because coping with violent death can be stressful, parents need to be encouraged to use stress-relieving strategies. Healthy, less stressed parents are often better able to help their child, and parents are often in a position to encourage their child and other family members to engage in healthy living. Facilitators may want to end the group session with a deep breathing exercise, a meditation, or a brainstorming exercise about things parents can do to relax.

Models for Adult Time-Limited Grief and Trauma Groups After Violent Death

Drs. Shirley Murphy, Edward K. Rynearson, and Katherine Shear have each developed and conducted research on group interventions with adults after violent death. For more information about their group models, see

1. Rynearson, E. K. (2001). *Retelling violent death*. Philadelphia: Brunner-Routledge, or for more information visit http://www.vdbs.org.

2. Shirley, M. (1997). A bereavement intervention for parents following the sudden, violent deaths of their 12- to 28-year-old children: Description and applications to clinical practice. *Canadian Journal of Nursing Research, 29*, 51–72, or Murphy, S. A., Dimond, M., Baugher, R., Lohan, J., Scheideman, J., Heerwagen, J., Johnson, C., Tillery, L., & Grover, M. (1996). Parents' evaluation of a preventative intervention following the violent deaths of their children. *Death Studies, 20*, 453–468. Dr. Murphy can be contacted at (206) 543–8569 or samurphy@u.washington.edu.

3. For Dr. Katherine Shear's group protocol, contact The Panic Anxiety and Traumatic Grief Program, Western Psychiatric Institute and Clinic, (412) 624–5500.

Facilitators Parent Group Outline for: "Reactions, Responses, Resources and Relaxation"

I. Introduction (5 minutes) _____
_____
_____

II. Reactions: Effects of Violent Death on Adolescents (15 minutes)

    A. Adolescents' reactions to violent death _____
_____
_____

    B. Traumatic responses _____
_____
_____

    C. Signs to look for _____
_____
_____

    D. Specific information _____
_____
_____

III. Responding: Ways to Help Adolescents Cope (15 minutes)

    A. Discuss ways that parents can help adolescents after violent death _____
_____
_____

    B. Benefits of grief and trauma group _____
_____
_____

IV. Discussion: Questions and Answers (15 minutes)
_____
_____
_____

V. Resources and Relaxation (10 minutes)
_____
_____
_____
_____

Helping Adolescents:
When Traumatic Reactions Interfere With Grief

After violent death, some adolescents may experience traumatic reactions, whether they witnessed the death or not. It is common for some traumatic symptoms to occur soon after the death, but if the traumatic reactions continue for more than a month, these symptoms may significantly interfere with the young person's ability to grieve. Adolescents who experience certain traumatic symptoms that occur for more than a month and that cause significant impairment in their daily life may be experiencing what is known as posttraumatic stress disorder (also called PTSD). Whether the adolescent experiences a few traumatic symptoms or has all of the symptoms of PTSD, traumatic reactions can interfere with the bereavement process and this is called traumatic grief. In order for the bereavement process to proceed as necessary, traumatic symptoms need to be decreased.

Adolescents who witness violent death or a life-threatening event are most at risk for developing PTSD. PTSD can cause significant problems in daily functioning such as school performance or problems with family members or peers. Also, PTSD in adolescents has been associated with other types of problems such as depression, substance abuse and engaging in other high-risk behaviors.

Traumatic symptoms can intensify or delay normal grief reactions. The reactions that are common to both, such as anxiety, irritability, emotional pain, loss of energy, sleep difficulty, and difficulty concentrating may worsen. Since many traumatic symptoms are internal experiences, such as intrusive thoughts of the violent event, flashbacks or nightmares, it may be difficult for parents and others to know by observation if the adolescent is experiencing traumatic symptoms. One of the first steps for helping adolescents who may be experiencing traumatic symptoms after violent death is for parents and adolescents to be educated about grief, trauma and PTSD. Sometimes adolescents may not share with their parents all that they are experiencing for fear of burdening their parents. Therefore, even when parents do ask their child directly about their thoughts and feelings, the young person may not tell everything that they are experiencing. Parents need to try to talk with their child about these experiences and give clear messages that it is okay to talk and share.

Parents are not immune to PTSD or traumatic grief. PTSD and traumatic grief can occur with people of all ages - from the very young to the very old - who experience traumatic events such as witnessing a violent death or having a loved one die violently. If parents or their adolescent or any of their family members are experiencing traumatic symptoms after a violent death, it may be necessary to seek an evaluation from a mental health professional.

**HERE ARE SOME TRAUMATIC REACTIONS
THAT MAY INTERFERE WITH THE BEREAVEMENT PROCESS:**

- *Thoughts, images, or perceptions of the violence and/or death return even when one does not want to think about it.*
- *Having experiences (feelings, thoughts) as though the violence or death or aspects of the death are occurring all over again.*
- *Avoidance of reminders of the violent death or the loss: avoidance of conversations, feelings, photographs, people, places or activities that remind one of the death and loss.*
- *Not caring about or expecting to have a future.*
- *Not enjoying things that one used to enjoy before the death.*
- *Feeling guilty for not being able to prevent the death.*

How Do I Know If My Teenager Needs Help?

When an adolescent experiences the death of someone close and/or witnesses a violent death, it is common for intense feelings and reactions to emerge. However, when the adolescent is suffering and experiencing depression, anxiety, posttraumatic stress or other problems that interfere with functioning, it may be necessary to seek professional help from a mental health specialist. Be aware of the warning signs that help is needed.

WARNING SIGNS:

1. *Stays by one self more often since the death, and/or seems withdrawn*

2. *Does not ever want to talk about what happened or the deceased, avoids reminders*

3. *Grades have significantly dropped*

4. *Change in attitude — doesn't seem to care, has negative thoughts about life*

5. *Change in temperament — more irritable, hostile, angry, quick tempered, withdrawn*

6. *Change in appetite or in weight — eating more or eating less*

7. *Sleeping problems — difficulty going to sleep or staying asleep or sleeps all the time*

8. *Does not seem to be interested in things that he or she once enjoyed*

9. *Uses alcohol or drugs*

10. *Talks about death a lot*

11. *Talks about wanting to die or hurting or killing self or others — seek help immediately if this sign is present.*

How Can Parents Help Adolescents After Violent Death

TALK WITH YOUR CHILD:

Teenagers need to know that it is okay to talk with parents and adults about the violent death and their loss. Sometimes youth may not want to talk about their feelings, but they may want to participate in reminiscing, telling stories about the deceased. Help them find ways to reflect and remember the deceased - tell stories about the deceased's life and allow the teen, if they wish, to add to the story or ask questions. Involve teens in memorials and celebrations. Consider planning special events during anniversaries, holidays, and special dates which involve the adolescent in the preparation and activity.

PROVIDE SAFETY:

Teenagers need to know that they are safe. You cannot always promise safety, but you can help create a sense of safety in your home. Teens may be embarrassed to talk about their fears and worries, but ask them questions. Talk about these fears in a respectful manner, in a way that does not minimize their concerns. Ask your child about revenge fantasies and give clear messages that while these feelings may be normal, acting upon them is not acceptable.

PROVIDE INFORMATION:

Parents need to provide factual information about the violent death and surrounding factors. Insuffient information can result in confusion. Provide honest factual information according to the teen's ability to understand. Allow and encourage questions and listen for signs of guilt. Teens may feel guilty that they did something, or failed to do something, which contributed to the death. Let them know it was not their fault. Teens may not only judge their own actions in terms of contributing to the death, but may assign fault to others -- explore this with them. While information is helpful, sometimes it can be too much especially when teens receive information from the media without discussion with adults. Limit the amount of media exposure about what happened. Sometimes the media exposure can serve as traumatic reminders, which may make it more difficult to cope.

PROMOTE AGE APPROPRIATE ACTIVITIES:

Guard against messages such as "now you have to be more grown up" or "you are the adult of the house now." It may be helpful for some teens to take on more responsibility after a death, but for others it may overburden them. Encourage adolescents to delay any major life decisions until the intensity of grief and trauma reactions decrease. Give bereaved adolescents permission to enjoy the things they once liked to do. Promote age appropriate activities such as time with friends, sports, and family activities.

TAKE CARE:

Adolescents need nurturing and care. No matter how old your teenager is, let them know that you love them and offer hugs. In an attempt to reduce stress, encourage healthy eating, proper rest and exercise, and limit caffeine. If the adolescent is abusing alcohol or other substances, seek treatment. Remember healthy parents are better able to help adolescents - if you need help coping, seek support and find additional resources to help you and your family.

Teacher/Faculty and Staff Awareness and Education

Importance of Teacher and/or Staff Support

Teachers and staff involved with adolescents who have had someone close die violently or who have witnessed a violent death need to be educated about the effects of violent death on adolescents. Equipped with this knowledge, they will be better able to understand the youth, provide support and identify those who may need additional help. This chapter describes a 1-hour educational group for teachers and/or staff who work with adolescents.

Having the teacher and/or staff group session in conjunction with the adolescent group may help provide additional support to the youth. Although the adolescent group members' confidentiality may need to be maintained, facilitators should inform teachers and/or staff of the importance of allowing youth to miss class or other types of activities to attend the 10-week group. The facilitators should explain that when youth are grieving and/or traumatized, academic performance might decline. Indeed, in some situations after violence and death, "symptoms associated with post-traumatic stress are likely to emerge in the classroom, where intrusive thoughts and emotional arousal may disrupt attention and where sadness, grief, and anger may interfere with the learning process and social adaptation" (Pfefferbaum, Call, & Sconzo, 1999, p. 958). Facilitators need to explain the benefits of the time-limited grief and trauma group for adolescents.

This one-time teacher and/or staff group can also be held with teachers and/or staff in the immediate aftermath of violence as a way to provide additional information about the effects of violent death on adolescents. Sections of this teacher and/or staff group format may be used even if a death or violence has not occurred, as a way to educate them should an event occur that affects adolescents.

Some studies (Schachter, 1991) found that adolescents identified teachers as a source to help them cope with the death of someone close, whereas in other studies (Hogan & DeSantis, 1994) adolescents did not mention teachers or any school personnel as being a source of support to help them cope. It may be that teachers and staff are not identified as supportive persons because they are unaware of the violent death. Perhaps when teachers or staff know who died too, such as a classmate, they are more likely to discuss the death and loss and provide support to bereaved adolescents (Ringler & Hayden, 2000). When teachers understand the effects of violent death on adolescents and are informed about a youth's experience, they are in a better position to provide support.

Although this 1-hour group meeting provides general information about the effects of violence and death, teachers and/or staff need to be asked directly about the type of information and services they need. Teachers and/or staff also need to be included in the planning process. For example, after the bombing of the federal building in Oklahoma City, a federally funded program called Project Heartland provided a range of services to the public schools. Committees were set up to discuss issues that affected the school community and to engage principals so these matters could be addressed. Some of the topics that the teachers and staff were trained in included: (a) the emotional impact of disasters; (b) effects of trauma and grief on classroom behavior; (c) holiday and anniversary reactions; (d) stress management; (e) expression through art; (f) impact of the trial, and (g) conflict mediation (Pfefferbaum, Call, & Sconzo, 1999).

Identifying Youth in Need of Mental Health Intervention

Teachers and youth staff who are aware of adolescents who have had someone close die and/or who have witnessed violent death can refer these youth to the facilitators who then can conduct further screening and obtain permission for participation in the time-limited grief and trauma group. Because teachers and youth staff spend a considerable amount of time with adolescents, it is important that they are able to provide support and resources and are aware of risk factors for mental health problems. As the teacher and/or staff group is limited to 1 hour, priority is given to educating teachers and/or staff about risk factors associated with suicide. Some of the warning signs for suicide may be associated with other types of problems, such as depression, posttraumatic stress, or substance abuse.

In a national sample of high school health teachers, most teachers (70% of 288 teachers) believed it was their role to identify students at risk for suicide, yet only 1 in 10 believed they could recognize a student at risk for attempting suicide. This is not surprising when only 21% reported that their school offered in-service training to teachers and staff about adolescent suicide in the past year. When teachers were asked, "Has a student(s) from your high school ever attempted suicide since you have worked there?" 59% reported "Yes," and when asked, "Has a student ever expressed suicidal thoughts to you?" 47% reported "Yes" (King, Price, Telljohann, & Wahl, 1999). Despite the prevalence of adolescent suicide and availability of suicide prevention programs, dangerous myths about adolescent suicide still remain. Acting, or not acting, based on such myths could have serious consequences. School personnel must be educated about the facts (King, 1999). Information about suicide is included in the 1-hour teacher and/or staff group since immediately after death some adolescents may have thoughts of suicide as a means to join the deceased or escape the pain. For most adolescents, these thoughts of suicide subside, but there are a certain percentage of adolescents who continue to have suicidal ideation (Balk, 1990).

Teacher and/or Staff 1-Hour Group Outline for: Providing Support in the Aftermath of Violent Death

The following agenda is to be used during the 1-hour educational group for teachers and/or staff. Handouts are available on the following pages. Also, a blank outline is included for facilitators to write their own notes for conducting the 1-hour teacher and/or staff group session. Information in the previous 11 chapters provides facilitators with additional information that teachers and staff may want to know. Facilitators may need to alter the format to address the unique situation. For example, when presenting to teachers after a suicide of a student, more information about suicide may need to be included. If a shooting occurred on campus, school officials may need to be included in the presentation to answer questions about school safety, or if a terrorist attack affects an entire community, more emphasis may need to be placed on resources and safety. There is a section in the group format called specific information that can be used to address unique concerns.

I. Introduction (5 minutes)

To lend support and credibility, it is suggested that a teacher or staff member who has authority with the group introduce the facilitators. Because teachers and staff are often extremely busy, facilitators need to remember to thank them for participating in the group meeting and present an overall agenda with the estimated time.

II. Reactions: Effects of Violent Death on Adolescents (15 minutes)

A. Adolescents' reactions to violent death

The handout "Reactions of Adolescents After Violent Death" includes a wide range of reactions that may occur with adolescents who have had someone close die violently or who have witnessed violence. Because reactions after violent death may vary depending on the adolescent's age and gender, a fairly inclusive list is offered. Inform teachers and staff that if these reactions do not subside soon after the death, intervention is needed. When discussing these reactions, facilitators should highlight some of the symptoms of PTSD and depression so that youth experiencing these symptoms can be identified. Facilitators may want to provide further information about adolescent bereavement (see chapter 3), PTSD (see chapter 6), and Traumatic Grief (see chapter 7). Facilitators need to point out symptoms that may affect the youth's performance, such as difficulty concentrating, difficulty sleeping, and irritability.

B. Signs to look for

Because many of the symptoms of PTSD are internal responses, teachers and staff may have a difficult time knowing if youth are having these experiences. The best way for teachers to "look for signs" of distress is to talk with youth and observe behaviors. When discussing the warning signs on the handout "About Suicide: Understanding and Helping the Suicidal Person," facilitators need to emphasize cues related to experiencing changes in behaviors. Specifically, it should be noted that sometimes the changes are not so obvious, especially for the youth who has had to cope with challenges such as chronic violence. For example, there may be a youth who has some history of fighting, but after the violent death when he gets into a fight he may beat the other youth to the point where medical attention is needed. This behavior should not be viewed as, "Oh, he always gets into fights," or "That's just how he is." It may be that rage from having someone close die or witnessing violent death has left the youth feeling out of control and having difficulty controlling impulses. Another example of a change is when a 12-year-old requested to see the nurse three times within a month because she was having headaches. The teacher sent the child to the nurse but never asked the child why she thought she was having so many headaches. The nurse and child finally informed the teacher that her mother had been murdered. After having this information, the teacher realized that the child had also missed several days of school and that her grades had declined. The teacher was able to work with the child to prevent her from failing. Facilitators should help teachers and staff to notice these types of changes in behavior.

C. Specific information

This section is designed to address specific issues and concerns related to the time-limited grief and trauma group and to the precipitating violence that the school community may have experienced, such as information about memorials, changes in class schedules, recommendations about what to do with the deceased classmate's desk and belongings, safety concerns, new policies, and so on. Officials and the facilitator may be involved in presenting this information.

III. Responding: Ways to Help Adolescents Cope (15 minutes)

A. Activities to Help

The handout "What Can I Do to Help Adolescents After Violent Death" provides a list of suggestions for teachers and staff. Discuss these suggestions with the group. Depending on the age of the adolescents with whom the teachers and staff are working, certain activities may be more appropriate. Facilitators should try to foster a discussion with the group about which suggestions they think will work best with their particular group and to share any other suggestions that are not on the list.

B. Benefits of grief and trauma group

If a time-limited grief and trauma group is going to be conducted, facilitators need to explain the benefits of youth participation. Teachers and staff need to be informed that while the youth's attendance may interfere with their participation in other activities, such as class, an intended outcome of the group is that the youths will be able to concentrate better and their functioning will improve. Facilitators need to remind teachers and staff about confidentiality and make sure that they do not announce to other students that the youth is going to a grief and trauma group. This type of attention may embarrass the youth and cause further stigma and feelings of being different.

IV. Discussion: Questions and Answers (15 minutes)

It is important to allow time for questions and answers so that teachers and staff can inquire about situations that may be specific to their youth. Facilitators may want to take note of certain themes that surface, such as how to deal with aggressive behavior, or teachers' and staffs' own grief and trauma.

V. Needs and Resources (10 minutes)

Let teachers and staff know what types of additional services may be available such as ongoing consultation, other educational presentations, and mental health services. Teachers and staff need to know where they can receive mental health intervention, whether they need help with past losses or issues, or as a result of a recent violent death. Facilitators may want to inquire with the administrators about insurance coverage of mental health. Also, similar to the parent group, teachers and staff need to be encouraged to practice healthy stress relieving activities. Engaging in relaxation exercises is particularly important for teachers and staff who also had someone close die violently or who witnessed the violence.

   If certain themes surfaced during the questions and answers section, facilitators may want to make teachers and staff aware of this and suggest additional resources to address the issues. Also, it may be helpful to leave teachers and staff with the handouts for parents (in chapter 11), "Helping Adolescents: When Traumatic Reactions Interfere With Grief," "How Do I Know If My Teenager Needs Help?," and "How Can Parents Help Adolescents After Violent Death," so that they can use this information and pass it on to parents who did not attend an educational meeting.

Facilitators Teacher and/or Staff Group Outline for: Providing Support in the Aftermath of Violent Death

I. Introduction (5 minutes) _____
_____

II. Reactions: Effects of Violent Death on Adolescents (15 minutes) _____
_____
_____

    A. Adolescents' reactions to violent death _____
_____
_____

    B. Signs to look for _____
_____
_____

    C. Specific information_____
_____
_____

III. Responding: Ways to Help Adolescents Cope (15 minutes) _____
_____

    A. Activities to help_____
_____
_____

    B. Benefits of grief and trauma group _____
_____
_____

IV. Discussion: Questions and Answers (15 minutes) _____
_____
_____

V. Needs and Resources (10 minutes)_____
_____
_____

Reactions of Adolescents After Violent Death

Adolescents who have had someone close die violently or who have witnessed violence may display cognitive, behavioral, emotional and physical reactions immediately after the violent death. However, if these reactions persist, professional mental health services may need to be sought.

THOUGHT PROCESSES

- Intrusive thoughts about the violent death
- Intrusive thoughts about the loss
- Difficulty concentrating (Note: grades or work performance may decline)
- Fear/wish of their own death
- Fear/wish for others' death
- Self blame — thinking it was their fault
- Blame others — assigning blame
- Unpleasant memories resurfacing
- Fear and/or doubt of the future
- Expectation of doom
- Difficulty trusting others
- Thoughts about someone else dying soon
- Thoughts about more violence occurring

BEHAVIORAL RESPONSES

- Increased need to control everyday experiences
- Tendency to isolate self from peers or family
- Avoids reminders
- Risk-taking
- Accident-prone behavior
- Clingy
- Argumentative with adults
- Not wanting to sleep alone or be left alone
- Afraid of going certain places
- Thrill or sensation-seeking
- Regressive behavior
- Substance abuse
- Truancy and/or tardy

EMOTIONAL REACTIONS

- Shock/denial
- Fear and/or anxiety
- Guilt
- Disorientation
- Hyper-alertness or hyper-vigilance
- Irritability and/or restlessness
- Outbursts of anger or rage
- Intense frustration
- Worrying
- Feeling detached
- Low energy
- Restricted range of feelings
- Self blame
- Shame
- Sadness/depression
- Betrayed
- Hypersensitive
- Helpless/Hopeless

PHYSICAL RESPONSES

- Headaches
- Stomachaches
- Digestion problems
- Diarrhea/constipation
- Crying
- Sleeping difficulties
- Nightmares
- Decreased/increased appetite
- Vomiting
- Sudden sweating and/or heart palpitations
- Easily startled by noises/unexpected touch
- Enuresis

About Suicide

UNDERSTANDING AND HELPING THE SUICIDAL PERSON

BE AWARE OF THE WARNING SIGNS

There is no typical suicide victim. It happens to young and old, rich and poor. Fortunately there are some common warning signs which, when acted upon, can save lives. Here are some signs to look for:
A suicidal person might be suicidal if he or she:

- Talks about committing suicide
- Has trouble eating or sleeping
- Experiences drastic changes in behavior
- Withdraws from friends and/or social activities
- Loses interest in hobbies, work, school, etc.
- Prepares for death by making out a will and final arrangements
- Gives away prized possessions
- Has attempted suicide before
- Takes unnecessary risks
- Has had recent severe losses
- Is preoccupied with death and dying
- Loses interest in their personal appearance
- Increases their use of alcohol or drugs

WHAT TO DO

Here are some ways to be helpful to someone who is threatening suicide:

- Be direct. Talk openly and matter-of-factly about suicide.
- Be willing to listen. Allow expressions of feelings. Accept the feelings.
- Be non-judgmental. Don't debate whether suicide is right or wrong, or feelings are good or bad. Don't lecture on the value of life.
- Get involved. Become available. Show interest and support.
- Don't dare him or her to do it.
- Don't act shocked. This will put distance between you.
- Don't be sworn to secrecy. Seek support.
- Offer hope that alternatives are available but do not offer glib reassurance.
- Take action. Remove means, such as guns or stockpiled pills.
- Get help from persons or agencies specializing in crisis intervention and suicide prevention.

BE AWARE OF FEELINGS

Many people at some time in their lives think about committing suicide. Most decide to live, because they eventually come to realize that the crisis is temporary and death is permanent. On other hand, people having a crisis sometimes perceive their dilemma as inescapable and feel an utter loss of control. These are some of the feelings and things they experience:

- Can't stop the pain
- Can't think clearly
- Can't make decisions
- Can't see any way out
- Can't sleep, eat or work
- Can't get out of depression
- Can't make the sadness go away
- Can't see a future without pain
- Can't see themselves as worthwhile
- Can't get someone's attention
- Can't seem to get control

If you experience these feelings, get help! If someone you know exhibits these symptoms, offer help!

Contact:

- **A community mental health agency**
- **A private therapist or counselor**
- **A school counselor or psychologist**
- **A family physician**
- **A suicide prevention or crisis center**

Reprinted with permission from the American Association of Suicidology
Phone: (202) 237-2280 website: http://www.suicidology.org
The National Hopeline Network 1-800-SUICIDE provides access to trained telephone counselors, 24 hours a day, 7 days a week.

Youth Suicide Fact Sheet

Suicide ranks as the third leading cause of death for young people (ages 15-19 and 15-29); only accidents and homicides occur more frequently.

Each year, there are approximately 12 suicides for every 100,000 adolescents.

Approximately 12 young people between the ages of 15-24 die every day by suicide.

Within every 2 hours and 2.5 minutes, a person under the age of 25 completes suicide.

In 2000, 29,350 people completed suicide. 13.6% of all suicides were committed by persons under the age of 25.

Whereas suicides account for 1.2% of all deaths in the U.S. annually, they comprise 12.8% of all deaths among 15-24 year olds.

Suicide rates, for 15-24 year olds, are 300% higher than those of the 1950's, and remained largely stable at these higher levels between the late 1970's and the mid 1990's.

Suicide rates for those 15-19 years old increased 11% between 1980 and 1997. Suicide rates for those between the ages of 10-14, however, increased 99% between 1980 and 1997. Both age groups have shown small declines in rates in the past two years.

Firearms remain the most commonly used suicide method among youth, regardless of race or gender, nearly accounting for almost three of five completed suicides.

Research has shown that the access to and the availability of firearms is a significant factor in the increase of youth suicide.

The male to female ratio (in 2000) of completed suicides was 3.7: 1 among 10-14 year olds, and 5: 1 among 15-19 year olds, and 6.2: 1 among 20-24 year olds.

Black male youth (ages 10-14) have shown the largest increase in suicide rates since 1980 compared to other youth groups by sex and ethnicity, increasing 180%. Among 15-19 year old black males, rates (since 1980) have increased 80% (2000 data).

Research has shown that most adolescent suicides occur in the afternoon or early evening and in the teen's home.

Although rates vary somewhat by geographic location, within a typical high school classroom, it is likely that three students (one boy and two girls) have made a suicide attempt in the past year.

Nationwide, nearly one in five high school students have stated on self-report surveys that they have seriously considered attempting suicide during the preceding 12 months.

A prior suicide attempt is an important risk factor for an eventual completion.

The typical profile of an adolescent nonfatal suicide attempter is a female who ingests pills; while the profile of the typical completer suicide is a male who dies from a gunshot wound.

Not all adolescent attempters may admit their intent. Therefore, any deliberate self-harming behaviors should be considered serious and in need of further evaluation.

Most adolescent suicide attempts are precipitated by interpersonal conflicts. The intent of the behavior appears to be to effect change in the behaviors or attitudes of others.

Repeat attempters (those making more than one nonlethal attempt) use their behavior as a means of coping with stress and tend to exhibit more chronic symptomology, poorer coping histories, and a higher presence of suicidal and substance abusive behaviors in their family histories.

Many teenagers may display one or more of the problems or "signs" detailed below. The following list describes some potential factors of risk for suicide among youth. If observed, a professional evaluation is strongly recommended:

* Presence of a psychiatric disorder (e.g., depression, drug or alcohol, behavior disorders, conduct disorder [e.g., runs away or has been incarcerated]).

* The expression/communication of thoughts of suicide, death, dying or the afterlife (in a context of sadness, boredom, or negative feelings).

* Impulsive and aggressive behavior; frequent expressions of rage.

* Previous exposure to other's suicidiality.

* Recent severe stressor (e.g., difficulties in dealing with sexual orientation; unplanned pregnancy or other significant real or impending loss).

* Family loss of stability; significant family conflict.

Please contact AAS for more information about youth suicide

Reprinted with permission from the American Association of Suicidology
Phone: (202) 237-2280
website: http://www.suicidology.org
The National Hopeline Network 1-800-SUICIDE provides access to trained telephone counselors, 24 hours a day, 7 days a week.

What Can I Do To Help Adolescents After Violent Death?

Teachers and staff can help adolescents who have had someone close die due to violence or who have witnessed violent death. Following are a list of suggestions for ways to support adolescents after violent death. After reviewing all of the suggestions, decide what approaches are best to use with the youth you work with and try them out.

- **Have a plan.** Review crisis response plans or policies related to responding to violence and death. Meet with administrators, teachers, staff, parents and adolescents to discuss the needs of everyone affected by the violence. Discuss implementation.

- **Establish safety**. If safety is not established, talk with youth about their concerns and work with others, including the youth if possible, to restore and create a sense of safety.

- **Make referrals**. Refer adolescents who are experiencing more severe reactions to a counselor.

- **Talk.** Create opportunities for youth to discuss what has happened. Know that youth may need to discuss these and related concerns again in the future.

- **Be patient.** Some adolescents may need more time than others to cope with the tragedy and to adjust to the changes.

- **Provide education to adolescents**. Have a mental health educator join you in discussing with adolescents common reactions to grief and trauma. Education helps normalize the reactions.

- **Maintain structure for activities and limits on behaviors**. Modify if needed temporarily, but slowly return to the expected schedule and rules.

- **Alter the schedule and provide opportunities for success**. For youth who are having difficulty concentrating, consider shortening lectures or activities, building in breaks, offering time to make up work, having more adults provide help in the classroom or with activities so that more individual attention can be provided, and/or provide tutoring resources.

- **Limit media exposure.** If the violence is covered in the media, limit the amount of time spent watching local or national coverage and always provide a forum for discussion afterward.

- **Respond honestly**. If you don't know the answers or are not sure how to respond to questions adolescents ask about violence and death, let them know you don't know or that you need more time to think about their questions. Find others who can help you respond to questions and situations.

- **Promote expression of thoughts and feelings**. Let youth know that having and expressing thoughts and feelings related to the violent death is normal.

- **Model appropriate expression.** Plan activities such as writing as a group a biography of the deceased, giving youth journals to record their thoughts and feelings, creating poems, songs, or prayers, or painting a group mural representing peace and hope for the future.

- **Help peers respond appropriately**. Ask the bereaved adolescent privately if there is anything that their peers can do or say that would be helpful for the youth. Talk with peers of the bereaved adolescents about being respectful and sensitive. Sometimes youth do not know what to say to someone who is bereaved or who experienced a tragedy — talk with them about this and provide appropriate responses for them to use. Consider having them pledge to one another that they will not say or do mean, disrespectful things related to what happened to each other.

- **Provide education to parents**. Provide information to parents about ways they can help adolescents after violent death. Let them know about some of the approaches you have tried.

- **Seek support for yourself.** If needed, seek support from a mental health professional, religious leader, doctor and/or friend about your own reactions to what happened. Know that prior losses and traumatic experiences may resurface.

- **Educate yourself about resources**. Ask a mental health counselor about available resources.

Part III

Preparing for a Group with Adolescents

A Note to the Facilitators

There are several qualifications and expectations of group facilitators.

Knowledgeable

Facilitators need to be trained in basic mental health interventions (Rando, 1992–1993) and be educated about bereavement, trauma, traumatic grief, and working with adolescents. Facilitators must keep abreast of new research and information about these topics.

Culturally competent

Facilitators must understand, acknowledge, appreciate, and value the culture of the adolescents in the group and be aware of their own culture, beliefs, and attitudes (Wilby, 1995).

　　If the population is one for whom English is a second language, it is recommended that a person who speaks the youths' "first" language be one of the facilitators, and that they be familiar with the group members' dialect. It will help the members feel more comfortable communicating their thoughts and feelings if they can speak in their native language. Also, if at least one of the facilitators is of the same ethnicity as the members, the members may be more forthcoming talking about specific rituals that are common to that particular group (Munet-Vilaró, 1998).

Concerned about prevention

Group facilitators need to know about and be involved in safety and violence prevention programs and strategies that work toward preventing violence and death. This will not only demonstrate and model a commitment to ending violence, but it may also assist the facilitators with preventing burnout since only working in the aftermath can be taxing. The facilitators can also encourage youth to become involved in community safety and antiviolence interventions, which can assist in their own healing process.

Utilize supervision

Facilitators must not only process the group sessions with each other but often supervision is required because of the complex, demanding nature of grief and trauma work and group work with adolescents.

Aware of personal effects

Facilitators are subject to countertransference, stress reactions, burnout, and what McCann and Pearlman (1990) describe as "vicarious traumatization." Vicarious traumatization occurs when the facilitator's views of the world, family, and friends become pessimistic and negative and when traumatic stress occurs because of hearing and observing traumatic stories (McCann & Pearlman, 1990). One can expect to be affected when working with bereaved and traumatized children and youth. At times, overwhelming feelings may emerge that need to be contained. Supervision and peer discussion is crucial for addressing vicarious traumatization (Lovrin, 1999).

Feel safe

"Therapists need to feel safe in their individual lives in order to be effective" (Lovrin, 1999, p. 116). As group facilitators work toward creating a sense of safety in the adolescents' lives, facilitators also need to feel safe.

Seek treatment if needed

Group facilitators who have a history of traumatic experiences may find that symptoms of PTSD may surface as their work with adolescents proceeds. Facilitators are encouraged to seek support and therapy as needed (Lovrin, 1999).

Guidelines for Group Facilitators

1. Be comfortable and knowledgeable working with adolescents.
2. Have experience facilitating groups.
3. At least one facilitator should be a mental health professional.
4. Be knowledgeable about adolescent bereavement, posttraumatic stress, depression, and traumatic grief.
5. Understand and have knowledge about the ethnicity/race and culture of the group members and be familiar with the members' environment or contextual influences.
6. Seek supervision, as needed.
7. Plan and process after each session.

Post-Session Review

After each session, the facilitators should discuss the following post-session review questions. It may be tempting for facilitators who have busy schedules to neglect to formally review each group session. However, post-session review can provide valuable insight into the process of the group, the progress of each youth, and the future needs of the group members and the group. Although this is a structured ten-week format, issues may arise that need to be addressed. Without the post-session review, facilitators may overlook critical concerns and opportunities for growth. Furthermore, without an honest review of the facilitators' own feelings, facilitators may inadvertently convey messages to the adolescents. Of course, it is appropriate for facilitators to model expression of feelings, but this must be done with the goal of helping the youth with his or her feelings. Also, because there are several youth in the group sometimes comments are made that need to be discussed further but are not because of time limits or other needs of the group. By reviewing the content of the group and each group member's participation, facilitators are more likely to remember comments and decide if and how an issue will be raised again. It is recommended that the "Post-Session Review" page be copied and placed where facilitators can easily use it after each session.

Post-Session Review:
Structure, Content, Dynamics, Progress, Co-leading Process, Reactions and Next Session

1. *Was the structure of the group session conducive to the group process (beginning, activities, ending, place, time, seating arrangement, temperature, noise, etc)? Are there any changes that need to be made for the next session?*

2. *What content was discussed/revealed? List all of the major themes that were discussed. Write down comments or issues that were raised but not addressed adequately. Will these issues be incorporated into the next session or is it best to wait until another session when that topic will be discussed further?*

3. *What group dynamics were present? Are there cliques or subgroups that are being formed? If so, how is this affecting other group members? Are there any scapegoats? Is any member taking on a role that may prevent them from reaching their goals? How is group pressure operating in the group? Is there a sense of group cohesion? If not, is the group working toward this or are there things that need to be done to try to encourage more cohesion?*

4. *What is the individual progress of each member? Name each adolescent in the group and review what he or she expressed in the session. On a scale of 1 to 10 (with 10 being "met") indicate where each is in terms of meeting the three main group goals.*

5. *How did the co-leading process work out? Did we follow and reinforce each other? Were there times during the group when one facilitator wanted to or did guide the group to another topic or activity when the other facilitator would not have chosen to conduct the group in that manner? How did this work out? Could it have been done differently? Do any changes need to occur in terms of how we are conducting the group together?*

6. *What are your own reactions (thoughts and feelings) about the session, including the content that was revealed or discussed?*

7. *Will the next session follow the group format or does it need to be modified?*

Starting the Group

Critical Logistics

The structure of the group must be carefully planned as it can greatly influence the process and success of the group. Organizing the group often takes as much time and planning as actually conducting the group sessions. Critical logistics and issues to be addressed when organizing a group include: parent, teacher, and/or staff education; outreach; screening; group composition; informed consent; adequate and consistent space; scheduling; and evaluation.

Parent, Teacher, and Staff Education

As discussed in chapters 10, 11, and 12, providing education to parents, teachers, and adults who work with adolescents about the effects of violent death and ways to help adolescents is an important component of helping adolescents after violent death. Facilitators who are organizing a grief and trauma group should consider conducting a one-time group meeting with parents, teachers and staff (group formats are described in chapters 11 and 12). These group meetings may not only benefit the youth who have already been selected to be in the group, but also they can serve as a way for adults, teachers, and staff to identify other adolescents who have had someone close die due to violence and/or who have witnessed violent death.

Outreach

Researchers have found that when conducting screenings with adolescents in schools many youth who meet criteria for posttraumatic stress disorder due to violence and death have never received mental health treatment (March, Amaya-Jackson, Murray, & Schulte, 1998; Saltzman, Pynoos, Layne, Steinberg, & Aisenberg, 2001). Many bereaved and traumatized youth are not likely to seek mental health services (Freeman, Shaffer, & Smith, 1996; Schilling, Koh, Abramovitz, & Gilbert 1992). Therefore, outreach must occur. One of the most effective strategies to reach adolescent survivors and witnesses of violent death is to offer grief and trauma groups at school where they spend most of their time and where a peer support group can exist. However, in order for mental health professionals to have access to youth in need of assistance in school settings, teachers and school officials need to be trained to identify youth affected by violence (Duncan, 1996).

In many community-based situations, community staff (school personnel, nurses, or agency staff) may identify youth they know who have had someone close die due to violence and/or who have witnessed violence. This is an excellent first step in the screening process as the community staff may be able to identify youth who may not have otherwise presented for services. Also, when community staff members have personal relationships with the adolescents and they refer them to the group, the adolescents may be more likely to participate. However, facilitators need to work closely with those identifying youth since parents and teachers may underestimate the extent of the adolescents' traumatic grief. Also, because traumatized adolescents may have high levels of avoidance, they may be overlooked by adults (Pfefferbaum, Nixon et al., 1999) who are not trained to identify these youths.

Sometimes, adults who work with adolescents may not know if the youth has had someone close die due to violence or if the youth has witnessed violent death. Therefore, it may be useful to use a brief, easy-to-administer assessment tool to learn about the youth's exposure to violence and experiences with having someone close die. The "Witnessing Violence and Death Survey" (which is included in this section) is an excellent tool to identify adolescents after violent death. This survey takes about 10 minutes to administer and can be given to a group of adolescents or individually. For youth who have indicated on the survey that they have witnessed violence or have had someone close die due to violence, a further screening session (as described in the next section) can be conducted to see if the youth may benefit from a grief and trauma group or other mental health services.

Witnessing Violence and Death Survey

Name: _____ Date: _____

Answer the statements based on things you have seen in <u>real life</u>.
Please circle the number of times you have seen the following:

	0 Never	1 Time	2 Times	3 Times	Many Times
1. I have seen somebody get stabbed	0	1	2	3	Many times
2. I have seen somebody get shot	0	1	2	3	Many times
3. I have seen a dead body outside or in my home	0	1	2	3	Many times
4. I have seen someone get hurt really badly	0	1	2	3	Many times
5. I have seen somebody dying	0	1	2	3	Many times
6. I have seen a crime scene after someone died	0	1	2	3	Many times
7. I have seen someone kill themselves	0	1	2	3	Many times
8. I have seen an accident where someone died	0	1	2	3	Many times

ANSWER BY CIRCLING YES OR NO

9. I know someone who has died due to an accident, suicide or homicide: YES   OR   NO

10. I have had someone close to me die due an accident, suicide, or homicide: YES   OR   NO

Adapted from Richters & Martinez (1990). "Things I Have Seen and Heard" Instrument

Screening

The main objective of the screening process for group participation is to assess if the adolescent has sufficient strengths and/or resources to tolerate being in the group without becoming extremely distressed due to the grief and traumatic symptoms they are experiencing. For example, if the youth indicates high to extremely high levels of posttraumatic re-experiencing symptoms and severe physiological responses and he or she does not have many resources and strengths, group work may not be indicated. However, some youth may indicate that they are experiencing severe traumatic symptoms, but they have sufficient coping capabilities and support from others so they may be able to tolerate being in the group. For youth experiencing extreme distress who are not able to tolerate group participation, a referral for other mental health services such as individual and/or family therapy and/or pharmacology may be more appropriate. It is to be noted that youth may participate in group therapy while concurrently involved in individual and/or family therapy or other types of interventions.

Due to the extreme traumatic responses and/or crisis state that the youth may be experiencing within a month after the violent death, the group intervention may be too overwhelming at that time and not meet his or her individual needs. Therefore, it is recommended that at least one month have passed since the violent death before the youth enters the group.

Youth may be screened individually or in small groups. Facilitators should select whatever approach is most comfortable for the youth. However, facilitators must caution against small groups if the youths do not already have positive relationships with one another. In this case, they may feel threatened, suspicious, and/or embarrassed and not return.

How do you screen?

The beginning assessment or screening must start from the strengths perspective, which is one that social workers often employ (e.g., see Saleebey, 1997). The strengths perspective assumes that when people's positive capacities are supported, they are more likely to act on their strengths (Weick, 1992). From this viewpoint, the facilitator can begin to determine the strengths and resources that have helped the youth thus far (see below for a list of strengths perspective questions). These strengths and resources can assist that adolescent in the group and help him or her cope.

During the screening process facilitators need to guard against the adolescent becoming too overwhelmed. Facilitators may need to guide the discussion in a way that attempts to minimize the youth experiencing extreme distress during the meeting. For example, if a youth begins to tell the story of the death and he or she appears to be in a trance (disconnected), facilitators should gently interrupt the story by asking questions such as "Now where were you?" or "Who told you this?" or make statements such as "If this is too painful for you now, please stop, and you can tell me the story at a later time if you wish." It is important to remember that the first contact is a time to engage the adolescent. Priority needs to be placed on helping the adolescent to feel comfortable.

Facilitators need to be familiar with how different ethnic/cultural groups may present and adjust their interactions accordingly. For example, when working with Mexican-American adolescents, facilitators may need to present in a warm, friendly, and informal manner when first meeting the youth. Facilitators will need to be aware of the Mexican-American concept *Personalismo*, which denotes a preference for personal contact and individualized attention in social interactions. Since many Mexican Americans are slow to disclose personal information (Ramirez, 2001), facilitators should not expect the Mexican-American adolescent to talk about the death, loss and adjustment immediately. Further, since many Mexican Americans find it impolite to disagree

(Ramirez, 2001), the screening questions should be posed in a way that does not connote a right or wrong answer, but rather encourages story telling about the questions being asked. Also, because Mexican Americans traditionally tend not to be task oriented, facilitators will need to educate the adolescents about the group process (schedule, time, and types of activities) (Ramirez, 2001). See chapter 10 for some resources about culture and bereavement.

Carlson (1997) in her book, *Trauma Assessments: A Clinician's Guide* provides valuable information about conducting trauma assessments. She states that the interviews should be therapeutic as well as informative. Carlson discusses some considerations when conducting assessments with traumatized people. Consider some of these suggestions when meeting with adolescents for the assessment/screening process:

1. Try to foster the client's sense of control before beginning the assessment process. Explain the assessment process before starting.

2. Let them know that they have a choice to participate and in what they share.

3. Inform them that if they get too upset to try and let you know. Try to monitor any discomfort, and if it appears that they are distressed, ask them.

4. Reinforce self-protective coping behavior.

5. Maintain a calm, accepting, and reassuring attitude and caution against underreacting or overreacting to the traumatic experience.

7. Toward the end of the assessment, highlight some of the person's strengths and coping capacity.

8. Consider providing education/normalization about avoidance responses, especially when they avoid traumatic content.

9. Be familiar with the special considerations of the specific population (Carlson, 1997).

Assessing Strengths, Resources, and Death-Related Factors

During the screening process, facilitators will want to assess the youth's support system, as one of the greatest risks is not having adequate support from the family and others (Worden, 1996). When meeting with the youth, try through conversation to assess if protective factors are present, such as the ability to maintain positive psychological connections with the deceased (Black, 1984) or the ability to maintain a balance of avoidance and reminiscence (Horowitz, Marmar, Weiss, DeWitt & Rosenbaum, 1984). Other protective factors and resources that are crucial include the psychological ability of parents and/or relatives to attend to the emotional needs of the adolescent and to participate in discussions and reminiscences about the deceased person (Horowitz, Marmar, Weiss, DeWitt & Rosenbaum, 1984; Worden, 1996), and the adolescent's ability to utilize or create relationships that promote discussion about the deceased (Clark, Pynoos, & Goebel, 1996).

During the screening meeting, facilitators will want to learn more about the violence and death and what this means for the adolescent. Therefore, after assessing for strengths and resources, facilitators will want to inquire about death-related factors. The following page includes questions for assessing strengths, resources, and death-related factors. Facilitators can use these questions as a guide for discussion with adolescents. Not all questions may be appropriate or need to be asked. The screening meeting with the adolescent needs to be conducted in a conversational manner rather than as a formal interview. Also, when asking specifically about death-related information, consider using some of the suggestions described in the section above (Carlson, 1997).

Screening Questions

Strengths and Resources:

1. What are some things you enjoy doing? Do you have any special talents or hobbies? What do other people say you are good at doing?

2. What type of things help you feel safe and comforted?

3. What has helped you so far to cope with the death? What do you do to make yourself feel better?

4. Before this death, have you had other people close to you die? And, if so, what helped you then to cope with your loss?

5. Who do you consider to be the most supportive for you? Are there other people who you trust to share your thoughts and feelings?

6. Name at least two people who you trust to talk with about what has happened.

7. Has your family been supportive? If so, who has been supportive? And how have they been supportive? Do they talk with you about what happened? What about your extended family, have they been supportive and if so, who and how?

8. Have your friends been helpful? If so, how have they helped you deal with the death and loss?

9. Can you describe one memory about **[name the person who died]** that you like to remember? Have you been able to share this story with anyone else? If so, who?

10. What are your goals for the immediate and long-term future?

11. Are there any other people or places or things that have helped you deal with what has happened that we have not talked about?

Death-Related Questions:

1. Can you tell me who died? Who was this person to you? How close were you with them? (If more than one person died, assess the type of relationships and try to get a sense of the meaning of each loss for the adolescent).

2. When did this occur?

3. Were you there when they died? If so, can you tell me about what you saw?

4. If the youth witnessed the death: Where you physically hurt? Was anyone else physically hurt?

5. If the youth did not witness the death: How did you find out about what happened? Who told you?

6. Did you attend and/ or participate in the funeral? Have you participated in any type of ceremonial events?

FOR CRIMINAL DEATHS:

7. Has the perpetrator(s) been caught, and/or charged?

8. What is status of the criminal investigation/ trial? Has a trial date been set or occurred?

9. Will you, or anyone you know well, be serving as a witness in the trial?

Risk Factors

If the youth has been diagnosed currently or in the past with a mental illness and/or is experiencing concurrent stressors from other factors in his or her life, facilitators need to assess if sufficient strengths and protective factors are present to buffer against the youth becoming completely overwhelmed and distressed. Other risk factors that could potentially exclude youth from participating include substance abuse and prior abuse or neglect, which causes significant impairment in functioning. When these types of problems are occurring, facilitators need to ask, "Is another type of treatment more appropriate for the youth?" During the screening process, facilitators may inquire about revenge fantasies and assess for any plans (assessment information about homicidal adolescents is included in chapter 8). Also, facilitators need to be familiar with the signs for suicide (see chapter 11) and assess for suicide if warranted.

What if the Facilitators Are Not Able to Gather all of the Screening Information?

Sometimes, community staff (such as school psychologists, school social workers, or school nurse) may conduct the screening, decide who will be in the group, and collect the consent forms. Also, there may be some circumstances where the facilitators conduct the screenings but they are not able to gather all of the assessment information due to limited access and time. When all of the screening information cannot be gathered, facilitators need to use the knowledge available to them thus far and ask themselves, "Does the youth seem like he or she could tolerate being in the group without getting too distressed?" Also, another question that may help facilitators decide about appropriateness for group treatment is: "Does the youth want to be in the group?" Facilitators can also use the information that the parents or guardians included on the Personal Information Form (included at the end of the chapter), which every parent or guardian is asked to complete before the group begins.

An Example of a Screening Session

Danielle, a 12 year old African-American girl, was identified by her school social worker to participate in a time-limited grief and trauma group to be held at the school. The school social worker administered the Witnessing Violence and Death Survey (located in this chapter after the Outreach section). On the survey, Danielle indicated that she had twice seen someone get stabbed, had once seen someone get shot, had seen someone being beat up many times, and that she has had someone close to her die due to violence. The school social worker sent home to her parent a letter explaining the purpose of the group, a client's right and consent form to obtain permission for participation in the group, and a personal information form to gather more assessment information (sample letter and consent and personal information forms are included after the section in this chapter called Informed Consent). Danielle's mother signed the consent form, but did not complete the personal information form. The school social worker arranged a brief meeting, about 20 minutes, at the school between the two group facilitators and Danielle. Since there was not much time allotted for the screening, the facilitators decided to use only a couple of questions from the Screening Questions (which is included in this chapter after the Assessing Strengths, Resources, and Death-Related Factors section). While both group facilitators where present for the meeting (one was an MSW student in training), only one facilitator did most of the talking. Here is an excerpt from the screening:

FACILITATOR: *Hello Danielle, my name is Miss Alison (Miss is used because this is common in the school setting). I know that the school social worker has talked with you about being in a group and your mother signed this piece of paper saying that it is okay. We wanted to talk with you to see if this is a group that may be able to help you. (Danielle nods her head okay). Before we talk about some of the things you put on this survey (showed her the Witnessing Violence and Death Survey she completed with the school social worker), we want to learn more about you. Is that okay? (Danielle nods yes.) What are some of the things that you like to do?*

DANIELLE: *I like talking on the phone and playing the clarinet.... (We talked more about her experience with playing the clarinet. Danielle is not playing in the school band since she just started attending this school, but she expressed that she wants to play in the school band.)*

FACILITATOR: *Are there other activities that you want to get involved with here at school?*

DANIELLE: *I am trying to get into the peer mediation program, but in the fifth grade I got into two fights but only one last year. I would also like to try to be on the student council. (We talked about how she may go about getting involved in these groups.)*

FACILITATOR: *Can we talk a little about this survey now? (Danielle nods her head yes.) Can you tell us who close to you died?*

DANIELLE: *My uncle.*

FACILITATOR: *And how did he die?*

DANIELLE: *He was shot. He was selling drugs. He was in the house and stepped outside. I was sitting outside next to my aunt and this car came up and shot. My aunt pulled me off the porch when they started shooting.*

FACILITATOR: *When did this happen?*

DANIELLE: *About two years ago.*

Facilitator: *Did you go to the funeral?*

DANIELLE: *I went, but I sat outside with my Dad. I didn't stay long.*

FACILITATOR: *What has helped you cope with this?*

DANIELLE: *My uncle is the pastor at my church. He prayed on me. I cried every now and then, but he says God took him with him. I go to church every Sunday. (We discussed how this has helped. Danielle also reported that she talks with her father.)*

FACILITATOR: *Was the perpetrator caught?*

DANIELLE: *Yes, the judge gave him life.*

FACILITATOR: *Did you go to the trial?*

DANIELLE: *No.*

FACILITATOR: *You put on this survey (showed her the Witnessing Violence and Death Survey that she completed) that you have seen people shot and stabbed. Can you tell us a little bit about that?*

DANIELLE: *My stepmother stabbed my father once.*

FACILITATOR: *Did you witness this?*

DANIELLE: *Yes. And my aunt got stabbed with a pick in the leg.*

FACILITATOR: *Did you witness this?*

DANIELLE: *Yes.*

(Since the Personal Information Form did not indicate if Danielle had ever been in counseling before, the facilitator asked her.)

FACILITATOR: *Danielle, have you ever seen a counselor before?*

DANIELLE: *When I was younger I was in a group with a social worker and other girls because I was molested.*

FACILITATOR: *Was the group helpful or not?*

DANIELLE: *Yeah, it was.*

FACILITATOR: *We know that we have asked you a lot of questions and you have done a really nice job talking with us. One more question? (Danielle smiles and says it's okay to ask one more question).*

FACILITATOR: *What are some of your plans for your future?*

DANIELLE: *(replying assertively) I want to be a lawyer.*

(After talking a bit more with Danielle and answering her questions about the group such as when it would meet, we told her that we would get back to her in a couple of days.)

Despite the tremendous amount of violence that Danielle had witnessed and the past sexual abuse she had experienced, she had a lot of strengths and resources indicating that she would be appropriate for group participation. Her family support, religion, current activities, desire to be involved in school programs, and plans for her future were indications of her strengths. Danielle was selected to participate in the group and was given the weekly schedule. She actively participated in the group and was able to write and talk about the violence she had witnessed and about missing her uncle.

Using Assessment Scales

During the screening process, facilitators may want to use assessment scales to ascertain the youth's level of posttraumatic stress and/or traumatic grief. However, facilitators who administer assessment instruments in the first meeting with the adolescent must be skilled in engaging adolescents and administering psychological instruments since some adolescents may feel threatened by the idea of completing a "test" about their experience of a violent death. As previously stated, while the first meeting is to assess for appropriateness of group intervention, it is also an opportunity to ease the youth's fears about participating in the group. Therefore, facilitators are encouraged to use their clinical judgment if an assessment scale will be used in the first meeting.

Assessment measurements are an important tool for evaluating if the group intervention has been effective for the adolescents. A subjective evaluation is not enough. Pre- and post-assessments are recommended. Measurements will not only give some indication about the effectiveness of the group, but it will also assist the facilitators in making any future recommendations for the adolescent. The next section will discuss the assessment instruments and evaluation. How the evaluation will be conducted should be carefully planned before the group work begins.

Evaluation

As stated in the screening section, it is important to have an objective measure as to the effectiveness of the intervention. This will also assist the facilitators in deciding if further recommendations for services are needed for the youth after the completion of the group. Also, as discussed in chapter 2, results regarding the efficacy of the group intervention can be used to learn about what works and what needs improvement, and to obtain grants and funding to provide group intervention to other youth.

Facilitators who are knowledgeable about research and the use of measures may wish to use

Screening Checklist

❑ *Has the youth had someone close die and/or witnessed a violent death?*

❑ *Assess the strengths and resources of the youth and capability to participate in the group without becoming too overwhelmed.*

❑ *Assess level of distress (including traumatic grief reactions) and risk factors.*

❑ *Inform other family members, if needed, about resources to assist them with the violent death of their loved one.*

❑ *Safeguard against the youth disclosing too much about what happened (and becoming overwhelmed) in the initial screening.*

❑ *Engage (establish rapport) with the youth.*

❑ *Have parent/guardian complete the Personal Information Form and the Clients' Rights Policy and Consent Form.*

❑ *Select measurements for evaluation.*

several methods such as report cards, parental observations, parent and teacher reports, and child self-reports to explore various outcomes such as depression, anxiety, or academic performance. However, it is recommended that all facilitators use at least one standardized assessment scale for adolescent posttraumatic stress or traumatic grief that has good psychometric properties (reliable and valid). It is also recommended that the selected posttraumatic stress or traumatic grief instrument be specifically designed for adolescents and easy to complete, and that the measure is culturally sensitive. Further, it is recommended that the group goals and the individual group members' goals be reviewed and ranked in terms of progress in meeting each goal (see Review of Group Goals handout in chapter 16).

Measurements

A simple self-ranking scale is used to assess the progress toward the following two goals: to provide education about grief and trauma reactions and to share some of his/her thoughts and feelings about what has happened. These goals are reviewed with the youth in the third meeting (see session 3 in chapter 16). Youth are also encouraged to set individual goals as well. Facilitators may need to help youth with formulating individual goals. For example, an adolescent having a difficult time sleeping since the death may include the goal of sleeping at least five nights a week without waking up in the middle of the night. Not all youth will establish a personal goal and the facilitators should leave this decision up to each adolescent. During the ninth meeting, all group members are asked to rank their progress on a scale of 1 to 10 in meeting the two group goals and their personal goal. If the youth is absent during that session, the post measure should be administered during the next session and/or during the facilitators meeting. (A Review of Group Goals form is included in chapter 16.) Facilitators will need to write each youth's personal goal on his or her individual ranking form. Also, it is highly recommended that this evaluation process be conducted during the ninth meeting (the second to last meeting) and not during the last meeting. If it is reviewed in the last meeting, youth may not put much thought into the evaluation, as he or she may want to quickly finish the scale in order to start the celebration (to eat the food). Also, if it is reviewed in the last session, youth may indicate that they have not made much progress in hopes of continuing the group and/or meeting with the facilitators.

To assess the first goal, which is to reduce traumatic reactions associated with the violent death/event, it is recommended that a standardized instrument for adolescent posttraumatic stress or traumatic grief be used. Since the field of trauma and bereavement is continually evolving, facilitators will want to select a measure that is current with the updated knowledge about trauma and bereavement. In addition, it is very important that the scale that is selected has been used with adolescents who have experienced a traumatic death, as there are many types of scales designed for different types of trauma, such as sexual abuse or child neglect. To obtain standardized instruments regarding posttraumatic stress or traumatic grief, contact the following sources:

- The National Center for Child Traumatic Stress, 11150 Olympic Blvd., Suite 770, Los Angeles, CA 90064, (310) 235–2633 or http://www.nctsnet. org and click on Search Measures Review.

- National Center for Posttraumatic Stress at (802) 296–6300 or http://www. ncptsd.org and click on Assessment and then click on Child Measures.

- Child Trauma Institute at http://www.childtrauma.com and click on Assessment and then click on Measures.

Facilitators should not use the results of the measurements to diagnose the adolescents, as such conclusions would be inappropriate. Determining a psychiatric diagnosis is often based on multiple sources of information rather than one test. In addition, diagnoses are only given after a trained mental health clinician has conducted a thorough assessment, and often such an assessment is not conducted for participation in the group intervention.

Once a scale has been chosen, facilitators should conduct research to learn if the scale has ever been used with the specific racial/ethnic population of adolescent survivors who will be in the group. However, even if the scale has not been specifically tested with the population in the group, it must not be assumed that the measure is biased just because it has not been tested for reliability and validity with the specific population (Knight & Hill, 1998). But, facilitators must be aware of certain biases that may occur. Following are a few points to consider when using assessment scales with different groups.

❑ Are the adolescents in the group familiar with the terms used on the scale?

❑ Do the questions on the scale have the same meanings for the group participants as the researchers intended the items to mean?

❑ Do the participants need the questions read aloud so that reading difficulties/learning disabilities do not interfere with completing the measure?

❑ Does language create a barrier? Many Latinos are fluent in both English and Spanish, and they may use English in public environments and Spanish at home. It is suggested that the measures used take into account the specific language and dialect of the group (Knight & Hill, 1998).

Facilitators will want to learn about administering the scale either by reading a guide to administration or through training that may be offered. Learning as much as possible about the administration of the scale is important, as there are numerous biases that can occur, such as the method of the interview, experience and style of the interviewer, the child's understanding and perception, and wording and placement of questions (Nader, 1997).

Administering The Standardized Scale

Usually the standardized scale to assess the traumatic reactions is administered in the second group meeting. (If the adolescents are comfortable taking the survey it can be administered in the screening session.) When administering the scale during the group, facilitators should inform the group members in the first session about the survey they will be asked to complete in the next meeting. Facilitators need to make it clear that this is not a "test," but that by answering the questions, facilitators will have a better understanding of how they are doing and will be better able to help them.

Facilitators must maintain a calm, supportive, and non-judgmental attitude when administering the assessment scale. It is recommended that the participants be separated when completing the scale and asked to not compare with their peers. The same scale is administered again in the ninth meeting (see session 9) as a posttest. Facilitators should take note when administering the scale (at pre and post) of any influencing factors that may have interfered with the youth responding accurately and/or that may have affected the results.

Group Composition

Eight to 10 group members are recommended, although groups can be conducted with fewer members. Factors to consider when determining the group composition include gender, age, grade level, maturity level, intellectual functioning, and type of violence. If both males and females have been identified to be in the group, it is important that there is a fairly equal number. For example, if only one male is identified or vice versa, this individual should be seen individually or placed in another youth group with an appropriate gender ratio. It is also recommended that the group be co-facilitated by one male and one female counselor, although due to limited resources this is not always possible.

The group members' relationships to the deceased may vary. For example, one youth in the group may have had his father killed, while another youth had a close friend die or it may be classmates who had peer(s) die. It is recommended that the type of violence experienced be as homogeneous as possible, such as suicide, accidents, homicides, or witnesses of violent death. The same type of violence experienced is not a requirement but it does allow for more in-depth information about specific topics, such as the criminal justice process, to be discussed when all youth have had a similar experience. Further, if the group is being held in an area where there are turf issues or gangs among the adolescents, it is important for facilitators to be aware of this and make sure that the selected group members are from the same area (turf) or at least not from conflicting groups. If the youth already has trust issues with other group members who represent an opposing subgroup, they should not be placed in the same therapy group, as 10 weeks may not be long enough to address past/current issues of trust. Such conflict between group members may interfere with the goals of the grief and trauma group.

It is best to have group members of similar maturity, emotionally, socially, and cognitively. As a general guideline, limit the range of years between the youngest and oldest group member to 2. However, age and grade level are not always good indicators of maturity, so there can certainly be exceptions to the rule. Having group members with similar maturity characteristics may enhance the interactions, discussion, and activities within the group. When there is a wide age range between adolescents, such as 12-year-olds and 17-year-olds, facilitators may observe sibling-like dynamics such as the older youth taking responsibility for the younger youth or not expressing their fears or sadness as a way to protect the younger youth.

Adequate and Consistent Space

Wherever the group occurs, there must be adequate and consistent space. In many inner city schools there is overcrowding and a lack of space; therefore, facilitators must insist on a designated, consistent area where the group can meet regularly. Having the group location change from session to session can be very disruptive for group members and facilitators. Consistent space helps create a sense of safety and confidentiality, two important factors for a successful group. Also, if the location is not in a private area, youth may not feel comfortable being in the group.

Group Schedule

If the group is being held at school, the times of the group session should be planned with a school official so that sessions are not scheduled on school holidays, half days or testing days. In addition, depending on the school schedule, the time may need to alternate so that the participants do not miss the same class every week.

Ideally, each session should last an hour and a half. However, due to school schedules or planned activities at youth programs, it may be that the group session can only be an hour. Facilitators will need to adjust the content of the group according to the amount of time allowed. For example, with an hour-long session, as opposed to an hour and a half, the general check in at the beginning of the session may last only 3 to 5 minutes instead of 10. Also, facilitators may choose one activity over another due to time constraints. Sometimes, facilitators may want to lengthen the number of sessions to more than ten to account for the shorter time during the session. However, if the number of sessions is extended, facilitators need to work toward ensuring that youth do not drop out due to the extended time frame. Also, facilitators need to caution against scheduling sessions with more than one week in between as adolescents may lose interest in attending.

Once the weekly sessions are scheduled, it is recommended that all group members receive a copy of the schedule (see schedule handout at the end of the chapter). Parents should also receive a copy of the schedule. If the group is being held at school or during some type of organized activity, teachers, school staff, and/or youth staff need a weekly group schedule as well. If members are attending the group sessions during an organized activity, such as school or an after-school recreation program, facilitators need to caution teacher or youth staff from calling attention to the group member when it is time for him or her to attend the group. Identifying the group member in front of their peers may cause embarrassment. Instead, group members can use their schedule to know when to attend the group, or teachers and staff can quietly remind them when it is time to attend the group.

Informed Consent

Whether written informed consent from the guardian is needed, all parties involved (parents or guardian and youth) should be informed about the purpose of the group and about the role of the facilitators of the group. Some adolescents may be old enough (depending on state laws) to sign the consent to participate without parental permission. Facilitators should be aware of school and legal policies regarding informed consent for treatment of a minor, as some schools include group counseling as part of general services and parental permission is not required. A sample letter describing the purpose of the group, along with a sample consent form, is provided at the end of this chapter.

Ideally, it is recommended that the facilitators meet with the parent/guardian to complete the Personal Information Form. It is helpful for the facilitators to gather additional assessment information about the family and the death from the parent or guardian. Information on the form is personal and if the person completing the form is also grieving, it may bring up intense emotions. Facilitators must be prepared for this and respond in a supportive manner. As discussed in chapters 10 and 11, the parent or guardian should be informed about and referred to additional services in the community, as needed.

Group Schedule:
For Adolescents After Violent Death

We, _____ will be facilitating a group at _____

_____. The group will be time-limited with a total of ten sessions. Sessions will be held once a week

in _____ room. Each session lasts _____. The group facilitators are _____

_____

_____. If you have any questions, please feel free to contact us at _____.

THE SCHEDULE FOR GROUP IS AS FOLLOWS:

SESSION	DATE	DAY	TIME
1			
2			
3			
4			
5			
6			
7			
8			
9			
10			

Again, if you have any questions or if we can be of assistance to you or your family please call us at _____.
Thank you.

Group Work For Adolescents After Violent Death

_____
Date

Dear Parent or Guardian:

We, _____ will be conducting a special group for adolescents who have had someone close to them die due to violence or who have witnessed a violent death. The group is designed to provide a safe and supportive environment for adolescents. Other youth who have also had someone close die due to violence or who have witnessed violence will be in the group. The goal of the group is to provide a place where the youth can share memories about the person who died and express some of their thoughts and feelings about what has happened. In the group we will do activities (such as talking, writing, drawing) to help the youth reduce traumatic reactions that started occurring since the violent death.

For your child to participate please sign the Clients' Rights Policy and Consent to Participate Form and the Personal Information Form and return it as soon a possible to _____
_.

Also, if you or any adult family member, relative or friend has had a loved one die due to violence or witnessed violent death, we would like to tell you about other services that may be helpful. Please ask us or call us at _____.

If at anytime you have any questions, we may be reached at _____. Please feel free to call us.

Sincerely,

Group facilitators

P.S. Please return the Clients' Rights Policy and Consent to Participate Form and the Personal Information Form. Thank you.

Clients' Rights Policy and Consent to Participate

We are pleased that you have agreed to allow your child to participate in the grief and trauma group for adolescents. As our client, you are entitled to:

1. *Ask about our professional qualifications, our fee policy, our policies and procedures and suggest how they might be improved.*

2. *Ask about our grievance procedure which entitles you to the following: If you have a complaint or are not satisfied with the service that you are receiving, you should first discuss this with the person who is working with you or your family. If this fails to satisfy you, please ask for an appointment to meet with that person's supervisor. No client who utilizes the grievance procedure to make a complaint will be retaliated against in any way. Our goal is to help you in any way that we can.*

3. *The group facilitators will make every effort to protect your privacy and confidentiality. Counseling services are confidential with the following exceptions. We are required to report possible child abuse, suicidal intentions or homicidal intentions to the appropriate authorities. Additionally, if your child is in some way involved with the judicial system, it is possible that the records of your counseling and/or your group facilitator could be subpoenaed by a judge, if these records are deemed relevant to the proceedings.*

4. *We will make every effort to respect each client's right to self-determination unless the exercise of such a right by a client occasions actual or potential harm to a child.*

5. *We will not offer services to minor children without the consent of a parent or guardian.*

6. *It is your right to refuse any services offered to you.*

7. *Know that sometimes case records may be reviewed by funding sources, medical consultants, supervisory personnel, researchers, and quality assurance processors for the purpose of evaluating services to you. In some instance they may contact you directly to inquire about the services you received and to verify information about your eligibility for counseling under the funding program.*

The Clients' Rights Policy and Consent to Participate has been discussed with me. My fee was set at _____ per session, or _____ for the _____week group sessions. I agree to pay this amount based on a schedule established with the group facilitator. We will try to provide you and your child with services of a high quality and to your satisfaction and we welcome your questions and suggestions.

Date: _____

_____

Signature of Parent or Guardian

_____   _____

Signature of Group Facilitator   Signature of Group Facilitator

Adapted from Children's Bureau of New Orleans, Inc., 2001

Personal Information Form - Page 1

PARENT/GUARDIAN (WHO IS COMPLETING THIS FORM):

Name:_____Relationship to child: _____

Address: _____ Apt. #: _____ Zip Code: _____

Home Phone:_____ Work Phone:_____ Other contact number: _____

Occupation: _____ Average annual household income: _____

Date of Birth: _____ Race/Ethnicity: _____ Gender: _____

Current relationship status:_____

Religious preference/church membership:_____

CHILD'S OTHER CARE GIVER:

Name:_____Relationship to child: _____

Address: _____ Apt. #: _____ Zip Code: _____

Home Phone:_____ Work Phone:_____ Other contact number: _____

Occupation: _____ Average annual household income: _____

Date of Birth: _____ Race/Ethnicity: _____ Gender: _____

Current relationship status:_____

Religious preference/church membership:_____

CUSTODY:

Who has custody of the child? _____ (please check type of custody):

__Joint custody   ___Sole custody   ___Guardianship   ___Foster Parent   ___Adoptive Parent   ___Other: _____

Family: Please include all persons living in the household with the child who will be in the group.
Put an asterisk * by the child that will attend the group.

Name	Relationship to Child	Age and Birthday (mo/day/yr)

HEALTH AND MEDICAL INFORMATION:

Information for the child who will be attending the group (Please include substance abuse information).

Physician's name:_____Phone number:_____

Has the child ever had previous counseling?   O yes   O no   If yes, where and for how long? _____

Has the child ever been hospitalized?   O yes   O no   If yes, where and for how long? _____

Is the child currently on any medication? (please list) _____

Please list any past or present physical/medical problems: _____

_____

Personal Information Form - Page 2

Has the child had a problem with drugs or alcohol?　　O yes　O no
Has the child ever witnessed domestic violence?　O yes　O no
Has the child experienced any type of abuse?　　　O yes　O no

EDUCATION HISTORY:

Current grade: _____　　Current school: _____　　Average grade: _____

Current teacher: _____　Other schools attended: _____

Special education? O yes　O no

Average behavior grade: _____　　Suspensions?　O yes　O no　　How many suspensions? _____

Describe behavior problems, if any:_____

SOCIALIZATION AND RECREATION:

Religion of the child: _____

What does the child do for fun?_____

What is the child good at? _____

Does the child have friends? O yes　O no　　Does the child have a best friend?　O yes　O no

How often does the child see friends?　O daily　　O 3-5 times a week　　O once a week　　O less often

Does the child have a girl/boy friend?　O yes　O no　　If yes, how long? _____

What positive attributes, abilities, and/or talents does your child have?

_____

What desires and/or goals does the child have?

_____

REASON FOR PARTICIPATING IN THE GROUP:

Please briefly describe the violent incident/what happened:_____

_____

_____

What was the relationship of the deceased to your child? _____

Deceased's name: _____　Age at death: _____　Gender: _____

Did the child witness the incident?　　O yes　O no

Was the child physically harmed from the incident? If yes, how? _____

Was anyone else physically hurt from the incident? If yes, how? _____

Date of the violent incident: _____　Date when the person died: _____

If there was a funeral, did the child attend?　O yes　O no

What has helped the child thus far in coping with the death?_____

_____

Please write any comments that you think may be helpful for the group facilitators to know when working with your child:

_____

_____

Thank you for completing this information, which will help us to provide better services.

If at any time you have questions or comments, please feel free to contact us at:

_____.

Adapted from Children's Bureau of New Orleans, Inc., 2001

Common Questions

What Do We Do When ... ?

This chapter provides some suggestions regarding common concerns that arise when conducting time-limited grief and trauma groups with adolescents. The answers to the following questions are only guidelines. Facilitators must use their own clinical judgment and seek supervision/consultation when specific issues arise.

What do we do when group members want to avoid certain topics and activities?

Because avoidance is one of the symptoms of posttraumatic stress, adolescents experiencing traumatic stress may try to avoid discussions and activities that are related to trauma reminders. Other adolescents may try to avoid the group activities because they want to talk about issues of more interest to them, such as who is dating who or new songs or movies. To keep the group focused on the grief and trauma content, at the beginning of every session facilitators should explain the plan and expectations for that session. Also, at the end of the session, facilitators should let the members know what topics will be addressed in the next session. Formalized discussion and agreement on group goals, as discussed in session 3, can also be helpful for keeping the focus.

If the session is an hour and a half, the first 10 minutes (during the "check-in" time) may be used for general discussion, although the facilitators will need to help the group transition to the focus of the session, or facilitators may allow the last 10 minutes of the group session to discuss other topics. Although facilitators need to maintain the focus of the group, facilitators need not be too rigid either. Facilitators need to allow adolescents to talk about some of the issues that are important or of interest to them. By listening closely to their discussion, facilitators may be able to tie the theme of the group session to their conversation. For example, if a youth wants to talk about new songs that are playing on the radio, ask if there are any songs that express how they feel about their loss. Also, when the adolescents are allowed "free time" to talk about anything they want, facilitators should listen for emerging issues in their life that may be associated to the violent death and help them to see the connections.

What do we do if an adolescent does not want to participate in the group once they already agreed and started?

Talk with the youth about their concerns about group participation. If the youth simply cannot tolerate being in the grief and trauma group, consider other types of interventions. However, the facilitator may ask the youth to try to attend a few more sessions (especially if the adolescent makes this decision in the first couple of sessions). Give all of the youth in the group the "right to pass" in the group discussions but have them try different activities that they may feel comfortable doing, such as writing in their own journal, writing a song, poem, and so on. Sometimes, having the adolescent simply sit in the group for a few of the sessions and listen to the others will allow them to feel more comfortable and want to stay. Acknowledge to all group members how difficult it can be to talk about what happened and offer praise when members share their thoughts and feelings.

If the youth still does not feel comfortable attending, a further assessment may need to be conducted to gather more information. If needed, discuss with the youth (and their parent/guardian) about being seen individually or in family therapy. Facilitators want to try to avoid dropouts, as it can affect the group dynamics. Many times, having some group members drop out cannot be avoided (in chapter 2, the dropout rate of the adolescent groups reviewed ranged from 0% to 18%). However, facilitators need to be vigilant about trying to minimize the number of youth who do not complete the group. Screening meetings and explaining to the youth about the process of the group is one attempt to prevent dropouts.

What do we do if members start missing the group sessions?

When group members are given the group schedule they need to verbally agree with each other and with the group facilitators that they will attend all 10 sessions. If one of the members has a conflict with with the schedule, facilitators and group members can try to rearrange that group session. Many times that may be difficult to do, but it does highlight the importance of every member attending every session. Having a couple of members miss one or two meetings is fairly common. If one member misses more than two sessions, facilitators need to meet with the member and explore why they have missed so many sessions. Active problem solving needs to occur to try to prevent them from missing any more sessions. For example, if the group is being held at school and the adolescent says he or she forgot the meeting, strategies about ways to help him or her remember should be developed.

What do we do when some group members have had more than one person close to them die (multiple deaths)?

Usually in the screening process facilitators ask adolescents about prior deaths and who died in the violent incident (single or multiple deaths). For adolescents who have had more than one person close to them die, facilitators will want to discern which loss causes the youth the most traumatic reactions and/or the most intense grief. When the youth is completing the pre- and post-tests indicating his or her level of posttraumatic stress or traumatic grief, the adolescents should be instructed to answer the questions based on the death that has caused the most pain and distress. However, the adolescent should be allowed to complete the group activities regarding any loss that he or she chooses. Hopefully as the youths experience the ability to tolerate and master the activities, they may try to complete the next activity or discussion regarding the death that is most difficult for them. If by the fifth session, the youth has never mentioned the most distressing death, facilitators may want to talk with the adolescent individually about avoidance. Also, facilitators should encourage the adolescent to try in one of the upcoming sessions to do one activity (drawing, writing, or talking) about the death that he or she is avoiding. Facilitators can also ask the adolescent if it is all right to ask questions about that specific person during the group discussions. However, facilitators should be careful not to push the adolescent too much. The adolescent's paces and rhythm need to be respected, but gentle nudges such as encouragement or asking questions may be helpful for the youth.

What do we do when a parent wants the identified adolescent's teenage siblings to participate in the group as well?

As a general recommendation, only one teenager per family should participate in a 10-week group. If more than one group is being conducted, consider separating the siblings. If only one 10-week group is available, discuss with the parent and teenagers concerns about the siblings both participating in the group and discuss if any other options, such as individual or family therapy, would be a better choice. Sometimes, having siblings in the same group creates dynamics that may prohibit one or both of the youth from getting what they need from the group experience. For example, they may not share how they feel for fear of being teased later at home or for fear of the other person telling their parents what they have said. Siblings may feel like they need to take care of each other and use their energy in the group for helping their siblings rather than focusing on their own thoughts and feelings.

The suggestion to have only one youth per family is only a guideline and there can be exceptions. For some adolescents it can be very comforting to have another family member in the group and it can be healing for them to share with each other their thoughts and feelings surrounding the death and loss. Also, they may learn in the group ways to continue to support each other after the group ends.

What do we do if another violent death or violent incident that affects a group member occurs during the 10-week time frame?

When incidents or events occur during the 10-week time frame that affect one or some of the group members, such as another death or someone being a victim of violence, issues surrounding the incident may need to be discussed in the group sessions. For example, if adolescents have someone else die during the time frame of the group, they may want to talk in the next session about their experience attending the funeral. Or, if an adolescent had someone close murdered during the time frame of the group, issues of revenge and safety may need to be discussed in the next session. Facilitators should allow for some flexibility in the schedule of group topics, especially when certain group issues emerge due to the youths' daily experiences.

What do we do when one group member has extreme stress responses and cannot tolerate other members talking about the death?

As discussed earlier, try to avoid having an adolescent drop out of the group. When group members are experiencing uncomfortable stress, facilitators need to provide education and normalization about traumatic reactions and focus on stress reducing activities. Facilitators may also want to consider having individual sessions with youth who are experiencing high levels of stress.

Facilitators can teach the youth individualized relaxation techniques and/or explore trauma content that is causing heightened stress. However, in an effort not to single out any one adolescent and have him or her feel like something is "wrong" with them, individual sessions, if they are conducted, should be held with all group members. For youth who do not necessarily need an individual session, facilitators can use it to check in with the adolescent and see how they are doing.

What do we do when an adolescent has an angry outburst in the group session and is aggressive (yells, pushes, or shoves) toward another group member?

Because of the intense emotions that adolescents may feel after a violent death, having two facilitators is a necessity. Also, having a facilitators' meeting after every session to review the progress of the group and each group member is essential (as discussed in chapter 13; see Post-Session Review). By analyzing each session, facilitators are more likely to identify tension between group members and potential aggressive behaviors of certain members. Early detection of anger, irritability, and aggression allows the facilitators to be proactive in helping group members control their behavior. Also, facilitators can use the other group members as role models for conflict resolution, problem solving, socialization, and managing frustrating feelings.

Facilitators need to constantly remind group members of the group goals that they established in session 1. Usually, adolescents set group rules, such as to respect one another, to not fight, and to listen to one another. In an effort to prevent displays of aggression, facilitators need to constantly alert members when they are not following the rules and encourage group members to remind each other about the rules.

If a group member has an angry outburst in the group, facilitators need to examine the precipitating factors and help the youth identify those factors. If aggression occurs during a session, facilitators need to end whatever group activity is being conducted and immediately stop the behavior. Clear messages, both verbally and through the facilitators' behavior, need to signify that such behavior cannot be allowed, because the group must be a safe place for all members. Facilitators need to discuss the incident with the individual members involved in the altercation and try to solve the problem. Also, the incident may need to be discussed with the group.

Part IV

Facilitating a 10-Week Grief and Trauma Group

A 10-Week Group Therapy Model for Adolescents After Violent Death

The grief and trauma group format is based on research regarding adolescent bereavement (chapter 3), bereavement theory (chapter 4), group theory (chapter 5), traumatic stress (chapters 6 and 7), violent death (chapters 8 and 9), and practice experience. The topics and activities are designed to establish a comfortable pace for the group members and to help the group members attain the three main group goals (discussed in chapter 2). Table 2 provides an overview of the grief and trauma group model.

Table 2. Time limited-10-Week- Grief and Trauma Adolescent Group Model

Goals: 1. To reduce traumatic reactions associated with the violent death.   2. To provide education about grief and trauma reactions.
3. To offer a safe environment for the youth to share some of his/her thoughts and feelings.

Bereavement Tasks	Stages of Group	Session Number	Session Topics
Early Phase (1–3)	Orientation-	1	Introduction, Orientation, Identify supports, Share nature of relationship of the deceased and/or Briefly describe violence witnessed
Understanding/ Self Protection	Inclusion (1–2)	2	Administer preassessment test, Educate about reactions to violence, Briefly share how the person died, Explore who that person was to the youth
	Uncertainty-	3	Formalize goals of the group, Provide grief and trauma education
	Exploration (3–4)	4	Recognize types of losses, Identify past coping techniques, List different ways of coping and help youth to find creative healthy ways to cope, Begin teaching relaxation techniques
Middle Phase (5–7)	Mutuality (5–8)	5	Discuss issues of safety and ways to feel safe, Identify occurring traumatic reactions, Explore techniques to decrease traumatic reactions, Teach relaxation techniques
Acceptance/ Reworking	Goal Achievement	6	Identify feelings, Maintaining Connections, Special dates and anniversaries
		7	Explore feelings of anger and revenge, Teach Anger Management, Provide Education about specific issues
Late Phase (8–10) Identity/		8	Identify supports, Compile a list of coping techniques, Discuss spirituality/religion, Examine family reactions and interaction, Explore sense of meaning in life
Development	Separation	9	Review progress of goals, Administer post-assessment, Discuss future goals and ways to achieve them
	Termination (9–10)	10	Recognize progress, Provide recognition, Terminate

Adapted from Salloum and Vincent (1998).

Activities and Themes for Each Session

It is important to have a variety of activities that utilize different modes of expression, as youth may receive, process, and express information differently (Corr, 1995). Also, facilitators need to be aware of youth who may have difficulty reading. If youth in the group have learning differences or disabilities, facilitators need to alter activities such that the adolescents do not experience stress or embarrassment. For example, facilitators should: emphasize that spelling and grammar are not important when writing a story as a group activity, read the instructions of a worksheet aloud to all participants and then explain what the sheet says, give choices regarding writing or drawing, and offer experiential activities that do not involve reading and writing.

Suggestions for Working with Youth Who Have Learning Difficulties/Differences

- Always read aloud to the entire group the instructions for a written assignment and then explain what it says.
- Ask if group members understand what is being said and what they are being asked to do.
- Announce that while in the group spelling and grammar are not important, expression is.
- Give youth a choice between writing or drawing.
- Consider changing some of the worksheets to activities that do not require the adolescents to write. You can have the youth role play healthy and unhealthy approaches to coping, use drama to demonstrate ways youth can identify and cope with anger, use a tape recorder or video and ask the youth questions about ways they stay connected with the deceased, use music to demonstrate how youth may feel keyed up or how they can relax themselves, or allow the youth to create a collage from magazine photographs of things that are important to them or what they want for their future.

Every session includes activities to facilitate expression surrounding a certain theme. The activities provide different means of expression such as art, writing, and music. "Art, writing, brainstorming, and written exercises all help elicit feelings, identify issues, and assist in resolving confused feelings and perceptions" (Hickey, 1993, p. 240). Facilitators are encouraged to use their own creativity when conducting the activities and sessions. Also, facilitators may consider inviting, with the youths' and guardians' permission, guests who specialize in different types of healing, such as a yoga instructor, poet, dramatist, or physical health expert, to teach and lead the group in a special exercise that addresses a topic.

Facilitators may consider giving each group member a workbook designed to elicit their thoughts and feelings about the violent death. Activities in the workbook can be addressed as a group or members can work in their own books when they have completed the group activity. When the group sessions are more than an hour long, having workbooks for individual work allows for everyone in the group to work at his or her own pace, whether that means taking all of the allotted time to complete the group activity or working ahead in the individual workbooks. If the facilitators are not able to afford a workbooks for each youth (although the books are fairly inexpensive), each group member should have available to them a journal/notebook that they can use to write and draw their thoughts and feelings. (See Appendix B for a list of a few recommended workbooks for adolescents after violent death.)

Session One

Topics: General introduction, Explanation of the purpose of the group, Identify supports, Time frame and structure, Confidentiality, Share the nature of the relationship of the person who died or Briefly describe violence witnessed

Opening Tasks

Introduction: During introductions consider using some type of general icebreaker. For example, have everyone say something about themselves such as what they enjoy doing; or after they state their names have them complete a sentence, such as, "If I were president of the United States, I would . . . "; or have them state their names and using the first letter of their first or last names state a word that describes them and starts with that letter.

Orientation: Set the tone and norms of group. Explain the purpose of the group and make known that all members in the group have had someone close to them die violently and/or have witnessed a violent death. Assess attitudes and tolerance of participants.

Acknowledge the difficulty of being in the group. Assure group members that the goal of the group is to help them and not overwhelm them; therefore, the group activities will occur at their pace. Inform them of what will happen in this session, and in the next session, and provide an overview of the future sessions.

Hand out a schedule of the group (see schedule handout in chapter 14) and discuss the overall structure of the group and the importance of attending all 10 sessions.

Let all members know that after the 10th session, facilitators will be contacting their parent or guardian to let them know the group has ended and to make any necessary recommendations.

Establishment of rules: Let each youth set one rule that he or she thinks will be helpful for making the group a safe place where everyone is respected. On one large sheet of paper let each participant write his or her rule. Add the rule of confidentiality (check your state guidelines about confidentiality and mental heath providers) and explain to the group the meaning and limitations of confidentiality. Discuss the importance of the rules, especially confidentiality among all group members. Have all members sign their names on the group rules sheet.

Activity 1: Share the nature of the relationship to the deceased or what was witnessed. Have each member say the name of the person(s) who died and include the nature of the relationship of the person(s) who died. For youth who witnessed a violent death and who may not have been close to the person who died, have them briefly state what they witnessed. For some adolescents this activity will be really difficult.

Guard against group members talking about too many details of how the person(s) died or about the violence, as this may be too overwhelming for many. Let the members know that there will be time to discuss and write about what happened. Also, it is important to inform members, especially in the beginning, that they do not have to talk if they do not want to (they have the right to pass), but that they are expected to stay in the group during the entire session.

Activity 2: Identify supports. Have each member identify at least two people they feel comfortable talking with about what has happened. Ask what their relationship is to these people. It is important for members to identify supportive people, as being in this group may bring up many issues and they need someone outside of the group to support them. Explain this to the members. Take note of any group members who cannot think of a supportive person in their life—they will need to be monitored more carefully as the group progresses. Also, sometimes youth may have people with whom they feel comfortable talking, but they may not want to share this with the group this early in the process. The topic of supports will be discussed again in session 8.

Closing Tasks

Ending ritual: Explain to the members that the group will usually end the same way, with the last 10 minutes set aside for a lighter activity. Ask for ideas about how they want to do this. This quick activity is to help moderate the distress level, provide containment, and help them transition back to whatever they are going to do next. Some ideas include members telling jokes, playing the UNO card game, listening to a song, and so on.

Remind members about the next scheduled session. Have all members verbally pledge to maintain confidentiality.

Session Two

Topics: Assessment measures, education about reactions to violence, briefly share how the person died or what was witnessed, and explore who that person was to the youth

Opening Tasks

Review group rules. Explain what will be accomplished in this session.

Activity 1: Administer standardized pretest assessment scale. See section on evaluation in chapter 14.

Activity 2: Provide education about common reactions to violence. The facilitators may want to use the questions or statements on the assessment scale to normalize the reactions to violent death. The facilitators may want to distribute the handout entitled "Reactions of Adolescents After Violent Death" (located in chapter 12) so that the youth can see that there is a wide range of reactions that may occur.

Activity 3: Briefly share how the person died or what happened. Let members choose which of the five worksheets (located after this section) they would like to complete. Giving choices allows them to feel a sense of control over what they are doing. In addition, youth who are not ready to express how the person died do not usually choose the worksheet "This Is What Happened." Youth who witnessed violent death may decide to complete the worksheet "This Is What Happened" or "This Is What I Saw." Facilitators should make it known that if the youth become too upset or distressed while doing this they can take a break. Inform group members that they can write or draw. Facilitators may need to provide encouragement and support, as some youth may be hesitant to begin this activity. Let them know they can write or draw as much or as little as they wish. Give sufficient time for this activity (20 to 30 minutes). Members are then encouraged to share their work with the group.

Closing Tasks

Before closing the group session, invite members to bring a photograph or something special from the person(s) who died to the next session. If members forget to bring something, remind them every session that they can bring a memento to share with the group. Usually, once one member brings something to share others will as well. This activity can be done throughout the 10-week time frame. Remind group members about confidentiality. Remind members about the next scheduled session. Facilitate the ending ritual.

There are many reasons why this person was so important to me. Here's why....

A Happy Time Together ...

A Favorite Memory...

This is What Happened...

This is What I Saw...

Session Three

Topics: Formalizing the goals of the group, Grief and trauma education

Opening Tasks

Review rules. Check in with group members to see how they are doing. Thank them for coming to the group on time. Explain what will be addressed in this session.

Activity 1: Ask if anyone brought a photograph or something special from the person who died. Let members share this with the group. If they forgot to bring in a memento, let them know that they can bring it to any of the sessions.

Activity 2: Formalize the goals of the group. Review group goals (see handout after this section entitled "Goals for Group") and purpose of the group. Have group members set one or two personal goals and have members sign the sheet.

Activity 3: Provide education about grief and trauma in a way that ensures active involvement of the members. Here are four approaches:

1. Review the handout called "Reactions" (located in chapter 12) explaining grief and trauma responses. Afterward have each member highlight in yellow the reactions they have been having lately and with a blue highlighter (or any other color) have them highlight the reactions that they had within the month after the violent death.

2. G.T. Card Game: Each member is given four cards that have the words *yes, no, sometimes,* and *question* written on them (make these cards by cutting paper the size of a standard card and writing the words on them). The facilitators state common grief and trauma reactions and ask if the participants have experienced them. The group members select a card and place it down to answer the question. This allows members to not only learn about common reactions but to visually see that others have experienced similar reactions. After each hand is played the facilitators can offer some education about the statement. If members want, they can add to the discussion or can place the question card on the table to ask a question. The G.T. Card Game handout is located after this section. This game may also be played during other sessions if time allows.

3. Weather metaphor: Explain that grief is like the weather. Sunny days, cloudy days, windy days, cold and hot days, rainy days, and so on. Discuss what thoughts and feelings would be associated with the type of weather. Have members draw what their weather (grief) looks like today.

4. On a large roll of paper (about four feet long) draw the "grief wave" (a wave indicating ups and downs) and label reactions under the wave (such as shock, calm, confused, angry, peaceful, sad, avoidance, nightmares, flashbacks, intrusive thoughts, etc.). Explain the different reactions of grief and trauma. Have each member draw a boat on the paper indicating what wave (reaction) they have been riding (experiencing) the most.

Closing Tasks

Before ending, ask members about the type of activities they enjoy, such as playing games, listening to music, writing, drawing, poetry, painting, and so on, so that the facilitators can incorporate these methods into the activities. Facilitate the ending ritual. Remind the group about confidentiality, when the next group is scheduled, and to bring a memento.

Goals for Group

This group is for young people who have had someone close to them die due to violence and/or who have witnessed violent death. Everyone in the group will try to make it a safe and supportive environment for you to express yourself. The group facilitators will coordinate group activities to help group members share their grief and reduce any traumatic reactions that members may be experiencing as a result of the violent death.

THE FOLLOWING TWO GOALS HAVE BEEN ESTABLISHED FOR ALL GROUP MEMBERS FOR THIS 10-WEEK GROUP.

1. To learn more about grief and trauma reactions.

2. To express some of my thoughts and feelings about what has happened

IS THERE ANYTHING ELSE YOU WOULD LIKE TO WORK ON DURING THESE TEN WEEKS? WHAT CHANGES WOULD YOU LIKE TO SEE FOR YOURSELF AT THE END OF THE GROUP?

3. _____

4. _____

_____   _____
Group Member   Date

_____   _____
Group Facilitator   Group Facilitator

G.T. Cards

OBJECTIVES:

This game provides education and normalization about grief and trauma reactions and other reactions after violent death. The game facilitates discussion by encouraging the youth to ask questions. It can also help increase group cohesion. The responses and discussion provides the facilitators with additional assessment information about the members. Cognitive distortions can be assessed and addressed within a group context.

DIRECTIONS:

Each member is given four cards that have the words yes, no, sometimes, and question written on them (make these cards by cutting paper the size of a standard card and write the words on them). The facilitators read the statements and ask the group members to respond by selecting a card and putting it down to answer the question. This allows members to not only learn about common reactions but to visually see that others too have experienced similar reactions. After each hand is played the facilitators can offer some education about the statement. If members want, they can add to the discussion or can place the question card on the table to ask a question. Sometimes youth find it difficult to sit still for long periods of time and want to physically move. Therefore, this game can be played by taping three cards on the walls in the room that state, Yes, No, and Sometimes. After the faciliatator reads the statement adolescents physically move to stand next to the card that represents their response. If the youth want to ask questions they may be instructed to either raise their hand or snap their fingers. This game may also be played by allowing the youth to make up their own statements to be read aloud, although it is a good idea to have the youth turn in their statements to the facilitator first so that the statements may be screened for appropriateness. Facilitators may want to change the order of the statements alternating from less difficult to more difficult statements. Also it is recommended that check marks be placed next to statements that need to be readdressed in another group session or individually with a particular youth. Depending on the time and amount or intensity of discussion, facilitators and/or the group can determine how long the game will be played during the session. If the group members like this activity, this game can be played during other sessions as well, perhaps with statements that address themes that have surfaced in past groups. The facilitators need to explain the game and let the group members know about the general content of the statements and that some statements will be just to learn more about each other.

REACTION STATEMENTS:

1. I have had thoughts or images about the death come into my mind even when I do not want them too.
2. I have had nightmares about the death.
3. I have had an experience where I felt like it was all happening over again.
4. I have had things remind me of the death, which has upset me very much.
5. I do not like to talk about what happened (referring to the violence and loss).
6. I try to stay away from things that make me think about what happened.
7. Since the death I have had a hard time concentrating.
8. Since the death, I have not felt like doing things that I once like to do.
9. I think that someone in my family or one of my friends is going to die soon.
10. Since the death, I feel very distant from people I once felt close to.
11. Since the death, I have a difficult time falling or staying asleep.
12. Since the death, I have been more irritable.
13. Since the death, I have noticed that I sometimes feel jumpy and get startled when I hear certain noises.
14. Since the death, I have been having a difficult time at school or at work.
15. Since the death, I like to be by myself more.
16. Since the death, I have not wanted to sleep by myself.
17. Since the death, I have had more headaches and stomachaches.
18. I have changed a lot since the death.

COGNITIVE STATEMENTS:
19. I am looking forward to my future.
20. I have plans for my future.
21. I feel like the world is a safe place.
22. I feel like I could have prevented or stopped the death from occurring.
23. I wish it was me who died instead.
24. I do not want to have children one day because the world is not a good place.
25. I feel like it was my fault that they died.

OTHER FACTORS:
26. I witnessed the violent death.
27. I was physically hurt when the death occurred.
28. I feel like my close friends really understand what I am going through.
29. I have family members that I feel like I can talk with.
30. It helps me to talk about good memories (about the person who died)
31. Sometimes I carry a weapon to protect myself.
32. I have had experiences where I have seen, heard, smelled or touched the person who died.

33. I cry when I think about what happened (referring to the death and loss).
34. I went to the funeral.
35. I want to go to the gravesite.

EVERYDAY THINGS:
36. I enjoy going to school.
37. **<Name a local school>** has a better **<Name a group such as football team, basketball team, band, etc.>** than **<name another local school.>**
38. I use humor to help me cope with difficult things in my life.
39. One of my favorite bands is **<Name a band.>**
40. I like to eat **<Name a food.>**
41. I like to play **<Name a sport or game.>**
42. I like to talk on the phone.
43. In town, I like to go to **<Name a place.>**
44. I have a pet.
45. I know exactly what I want to do for my career.
46. **<Name something>** that makes me feel good.

Session Four

Topics: Recognize different types of losses, Identify past coping techniques, List different ways of coping and help youth to find creative healthy ways to cope, Begin teaching relaxation techniques

Opening Tasks

Review rules. Check in with members. Explain what will be addressed in this session.

Activity 1: Share photographs or mementos if anyone brought them to the group. Importance of memories needs to be discussed. Again, encourage members to bring in photographs and special memorabilia.

Activity 2: Recognize different types of losses, identify past coping techniques, and list different ways of coping. This activity involves education and discussion of different types of losses and identifying ways the members may have coped in the past. Different types of losses include divorce, separations, changing schools, breaking up with girlfriend or boyfriend, and incarceration. Ask members to state different types of losses that they have experienced in the past. List all of these losses on a large sheet of paper. On another sheet of large paper, write the question, "What helped you cope with your loss in the past?" Have members state ways that helped them in the past and have one facilitator record all of the different coping strategies that were used.

Activity 3: Creative, healthy ways to cope. Using the list that was developed by the group members, have the group members decide if the coping approach is healthy or unhealthy. Facilitators need to elicit discussion from the group, especially about ways to cope, as different groups will hold different ideas about what is helpful and acceptable. Potential consequences of unhealthy coping need to be discussed among the members. Facilitators need to discuss that some coping approaches are often used as a self-protective means and may be healthy in one circumstance, but unhealthy in another (see chapter 9 about coping). The two worksheets "Coping After Violent Death: Healthy Ways" and "Unhealthy Approaches to Trying to Cope With What Happened," located after this section, can be used to identify coping approaches. Note: the issue of revenge and suicide will be discussed again in session 7.

Activity 4: Relaxation. When discussing ways of coping, highlight relaxation activities that may help adolescents and ask that they try one of these strategies before the next session. Also, facilitators may want to teach simple relaxation techniques such as deep breathing or muscle relaxation exercises (this will be discussed again in session 5).

Activity 5: If time allows, facilitators may want to encourage expression of thoughts and feelings by using one of the suggestions that members gave in session 3 (see closing tasks) when asked about activities they enjoy. For example, provide paper for members to write poetry or lyrics to songs that express how they feel. They can write or draw a dedication/tribute to the person who died. It helps to use interesting or "cool" graphic paper and/or to offer to type it with fancy fonts and graphics if they do not have a computer.

Closing Tasks

Inform members that there are 6 sessions remaining. Remind the group about confidentiality, when the next group is scheduled, and to bring a memento if they want. Close with the ending ritual.

Coping After Violent Death: Healthy Ways

- *Talk with someone you trust.*

- *Ask family members and friends to tell you about the person who died.*

- *Share memories about the person.*

- *Write your thoughts and feelings in a journal.*

- *Play a game or sports or exercise.*

- *Write a poem or draw a picture or write a song about the person who died or about what happened.*

- *Participate in a memorial or take flowers to the grave.*

- *Pray, meditate, take deep breaths, or go to your safe place when you feel upset.*

- *Learn about grief and trauma so that you understand what you are experiencing.*

WHAT ARE SOME OTHER HEALTHY WAYS PEOPLE MAY RESPOND AFTER VIOLENT DEATH?

_____ _____

_____

_____

BEING ABLE TO USE A VARIETY OF COPING STRATEGIES CAN HELP YOU IN DIFFERENT CIRCUMSTANCES. NAME AT LEAST FIVE WAYS THAT YOU HAVE USED OR WILL USE TO DEAL WITH WHAT HAS HAPPENED. PUT A STAR BY THE ONE YOU WILL USE TODAY.

1. _____

2. _____

3. _____

4. _____

5. _____

Unhealthy Approaches to Trying to Cope With What Happened

Sometimes you may express your feelings in unhealthy ways. While you may do this to try to cope with the death, these reactions may harm you.

SOME UNHEALTHY REACTIONS INCLUDE:

- *For a long time, not talking to anyone about the person who died or about what happened.*

- *Fighting.*

- *Smoking or drinking alcohol to numb the feelings.*

- *Not caring about your future.*

- *Making plans for retaliation.*

- *Wanting to hurt or kill yourself — Making plans for harming yourself.*

- *Putting yourself in dangerous positions such as driving fast and reckless.*

What are some other unhealthy ways people may have responded after violent death? _____

_____

_____

Have you used any of these unhealthy ways to deal with what has happened? (Circle one) yes or no

If so, which one(s) _____

_____

_____

_____

What are some potential negative consequences of using these approaches? _____

_____

_____

_____

Session Five

Topics: Discuss issues of safety and ways to feel safe, Identify occurring traumatic reactions, Explore techniques to decrease the traumatic reactions, Teach relaxation techniques

Opening Tasks

Review rules. Check in with group members to see how they are doing. Explain what will be addressed in this session.

Activity 1: If needed, allow time for group members to finish and share work that was started in session 4 (see session 4, activity four). Also, if any members brought a photograph or memento allow them to share this with the other members.

Activity 2: Safety. Have each member state again (this was done in session 1) at least two people they feel that they can trust to talk with about what has happened. Encourage them to talk with these supportive people. Next, it is important that the members can identify a place that gives them a sense of safety. If they cannot identify a place, then have them make one up. Let members draw about this place and/or describe what it is like in detail. The worksheet at the end of this section "Creating a Sense of Safety" provides an activity for discussing being safe. Many of the recommended workbooks also have worksheets that may be used regarding safety.

Activity 3: Identify traumatic reactions and explore techniques to decrease them. Using the pretest of traumatic reactions that were administered in session 2, facilitators should identify the most common traumatic reactions that the group members indicated they were experiencing. Discuss these reactions with the group members in terms of being normal reactions to traumatic events and provide education about posttraumatic stress. Facilitators may wish to have the adolescents read the handout in chapter 11 entitled "Helping Adolescents: When Traumatic Reactions Interfere With Grief."

Have each group member identify if they are having more reexperiencing, avoidance, or hyperarousal symptoms. Depending on which one the members identified as occurring the most, have them complete one of the following worksheets: "It's Like Experiencing It Again," "Avoidance: Pushing It All Away," "Feeling Keyed Up." Encourage the youth to practice one strategy for reducing the identified reaction during the week.

Activity 4: Relaxation. If the topic relaxation was highlighted during the last session, ask the members if they tried any of the strategies and if it helped. Continue to teach relaxation techniques, which can be accomplished in various ways. One way is to teach members how to utilize deep breathing as a way to calm down. Another approach may be to do guided imagery and have members return to their safe place. Other techniques, such as teaching ways to meditate, stretching to relax muscles, repeating positive thoughts, counting backward from 10, and listening to calm music, may be used. Sometimes, the issue of spirituality comes up when discussing relaxation techniques. Spirituality will be discussed in session 8, but if the group brings it up, allow for discussion in this session.

Also, in an attempt to promote relaxation and stress relieving activities, group members should be encouraged to participate in any extracurricular activities.

Closing Tasks

Announce that there are only 5 more sessions remaining and allow for comments and discussion regarding feelings about ending the group. Remind members about maintaining confidentiality. Close the group with an ending ritual.

Creating a Sense of Safety

The world may not feel safe. The way that you think about others and the world may be different now since the death. Sometimes after something like this happens people may feel fear and maybe a sense of helplessness. While things, including yourself, have changed, it is important to regain or create a sense of safety. Real, concrete measures can be taken to keep you safe. Can you list some things that will help make you feel safe?

_____   _____

_____   _____

_____   _____

Regaining or creating a sense of safety after such a horrific event may take some time. After traumatic events, many people have reported feeling nervous, jumpy, on edge, fearful and scared. One thing that may help you is to think of a person, place or even a thing that makes you feel safe. If you can be with that person or go to that place, it may be helpful. But sometimes that is not possible.

However, by actively thinking of the person, place or thing that makes you feel safe you can help rebuild a sense of safety and create a safety zone where you can go in your mind anytime you need to. Actively think about this person, place or thing that makes you feel safe. Think about where you are. Is anyone with you? If so, who? What are they saying to you to make you feel better? What are the sights, sounds, smells, of the things around you? How do you feel there?

MY SAFETY ZONE (IMAGINE, WRITE AND/OR DRAW ABOUT A SAFE PLACE FOR YOU)

```



```

It's Like Experiencing It Again

One reaction that may occur when such a traumatic event happens is called re-experiencing. This is when the thoughts and/or images about what happened come back to you even when you don't want them to. Or, when something reminds you about what happened and you feel like you are experiencing it all over again. Sometimes reminders, or "triggers," may cause you to have images, feelings, smells, sounds, and maybe tastes that feel like it was when it happened. There may be one thought or image that keeps replaying over and over. Even if you were not there when it happened, you may have reoccurring thoughts about how they died.

HAVE YOU EVER HAD AN EXPERIENCE LIKE IT WAS OCCURRING AGAIN?
CIRCLE   YES   OR   NO

HAVE YOU EVER HAD THOUGHTS ABOUT THE DEATH COME BACK TO YOU WHEN YOU DID NOT WANT THEM TO?
CIRCLE   YES   OR   NO

HAVE YOU EVER HAD A BAD DREAM OR A NIGHTMARE ABOUT WHAT HAPPENED?
CIRCLE   YES   OR   NO

WHAT REMINDERS OR "TRIGGERS" CAUSE YOU TO HAVE RE-EXPERIENCING REACTIONS?

_____

_____

_____

_____

_____

Not everyone will have re-experiencing responses. Some people may only have this re-experiencing happen once, while others have many re-experiencing reactions. If you sometimes have experiences like it is occurring again or have thoughts about the death when you don't want to, try some different things to help you when these reactions occur. Put a check mark by the things you will try when you have re-experiencing reactions.

❑ **IMAGINE YOURSELF IN YOUR SAFETY ZONE.**
❑ **DO SOMETHING TO DISTRACT YOURSELF.**
❑ **TELL YOURSELF, "I DO NOT HAVE TO THINK ABOUT THIS NOW."**
❑ **TELL SOMEONE ABOUT WHAT YOU ARE EXPERIENCING.**
❑ **START DOING SOMETHING YOU ENJOY.**
❑ **PLAY FAMILIAR MUSIC.**
❑ **ASK SOMEONE TO SIT WITH YOU AND/OR HUG YOU.**
❑ **WRITE OR DRAW ABOUT YOUR THOUGHTS AND FEELINGS.**
❑ **TALK TO YOURSELF WHEN IT IS HAPPENING, TELLING YOURSELF THAT YOU WILL BE OKAY.**
❑ **TRY TO REMAIN CALM BY BREATHING DEEPLY, OR SAYING A PRAYER OR MEDITATION.**
❑ **TALK WITH A COUNSELOR ABOUT WHAT YOU ARE EXPERIENCING.**

Avoidance: Pushing It All Away

When a traumatic event happens, many people simply cannot bear to keep thinking about what happened. They may try to avoid thoughts, feeling, conversations, places, and people that remind them about what happened. They may try to push it away. Avoidance can take a lot of energy and can be draining. Some avoidance may be healthy because it can give your mind a break, but when you are always avoiding things associated with the death, this may prevent you from healing and grieving.

DO YOU TRY TO AVOID THOUGHTS, FEELINGS, CONVERSATION, PLACES OR PEOPLE THAT REMIND YOU ABOUT THE VIOLENT DEATH?   **CIRCLE   YES   OR   NO**

If yes, try to write or draw about what you avoid the most? Sometimes when you are able to face what you want to avoid, you learn that you can handle it and you don't have to push it away. However, it is important to have a lot of support from other people who can help you.

WRITE OR DRAW ABOUT WHAT YOU AVOID THE MOST

Feeling Keyed Up

After a violent death you may feel "keyed up," like your body and mind cannot rest. You may have difficulty falling or staying asleep, be more irritable, have angry outbursts, have difficulty concentrating, or feel jumpy, nervous or on guard.

IT IS IMPORTANT TO BE AWARE OF YOUR REACTIONS. PUT A CHECK MARK BY THE REACTIONS THAT YOU HAVE HAD IN THE PAST TWO WEEKS.

❑ *Stomachaches* ❑ *Headaches* ❑ *Tight chest*
❑ *Heart racing* ❑ *Sweating* ❑ *Crying*
❑ *Low energy* ❑ *Decreased or increased appetite* ❑ *Irritable*
❑ *Nervous or jumpy* ❑ *Quick to get angry* ❑ *Temper tantrums*
❑ *Difficulty concentrating* ❑ *More forgetful* ❑ *On-guard*

WHEN THESE TYPES OF REACTIONS OCCUR, IT IS IMPORTANT TO TAKE CARE OF YOURSELF. FOR THE NEXT COUPLE OF WEEKS, TRY TO DO AT LEAST ONE OF THE FOLLOWING ACTIVITIES EACH DAY. THESE ARE SIMPLE THINGS, BUT AS YOU GO THROUGH THIS DIFFICULT TIME, THEY CAN REALLY HELP.

1. **EAT A BALANCED MEAL**

2. **EXERCISE: PLAY A SPORT OR GO FOR A WALK OR RIDE A BIKE**

3. **HAVE QUIET TIME: RELAX IN YOUR ROOM OR IN A QUIET SPACE**

4. **LISTEN TO YOUR CALM MUSIC**

5. **DO SOMETHING THAT YOU ENJOY**

6. **LIMIT CAFFEINE INTAKE**

7. **TAKE A WARM BATH**

8. **TALK WITH SOMEONE YOU TRUST ABOUT YOUR FEELINGS**

CAN YOU THINK OF OTHERS HELPFUL THINGS THAT YOU CAN DO TO TAKE CARE OF YOURSELF?

_____   _____

_____   _____

_____   _____

_____   _____

_____   _____

Session Six

Topic: Identify feelings, special dates and anniversaries, maintain connections

Opening Tasks

Briefly review group rules. Check in with group members to see how they are doing. Ask if anyone during the past week used their "safety zone," relaxation techniques, and/or tried any of the ideas for reducing reactions, and if it was helpful.

Explain what will be addressed in this session. Ask if anyone brought a photograph or something special from the person who died and let them share it with the group. Also, let the group members know that they have only 3 more sessions to bring memorabilia to share.

By this session members should feel safe enough to share with the group how they are feeling and to ask questions that have been on their mind. Facilitators can chose between activity 1 or activity 2 depending on which one they think the group will like the most. If enough time is available both activities can be done.

Activity 1: Identify feelings. On the big sheet of paper that had the grief wave (from session 3) write down the many different feelings that may occur when someone dies. If you did not use the grief wave activity, on a big sheet of paper (about 4 feet long) draw a rolling wave. On the sheet, include such feelings as guilt, sadness, shock, anger, depression, hopelessness, loneliness, revenge, jealousy, nervousness, numbness, irritation, and so on. Have the group discuss these feeling and then ask each member to identify the ones that they have felt since the person died. Members may want to sign their name by the feelings they have felt or draw a boat with their initials indicating that they have had or are having that particular feeling. Afterward, members may each draw a picture of the weather as a metaphor to indicate how they have been feeling lately. Sometimes this discussion can bring up intense feelings such as guilt. Encourage members to talk about how they are feeling or have felt. Facilitate group support of each other and comment when members experience similar feelings, as this helps reduce feeling isolated and "crazy." Note that the next session will allow time for the topics of revenge and anger.

Activity 2: Identify feelings. Have the group members complete the worksheet at the end of this section entitled "So Many Questions and *If Only* . . . " Ask if group members will share the questions they listed and facilitate discussion among the group. Also, ask if members have had "if only" thoughts and ask them to share them with the group.

If facilitators do not have time for both Activity 3 and 4, they may need to choose one.

Activity 3: Maintain connections. Facilitators may want to reread the section "Maintaining a Connection" in chapter 9 before conducting this activity. This activity is primarily for adolescents who have had a parent or sibling or very close family member die. If most of the members have experienced the death of a peer, facilitators may want to skip this activity. Discuss the phenomena of remaining connected with the deceased. Have group members complete the worksheet "Staying Connected" at the end of this section and ask them to share some of their responses.

Activity 4: Maintain connections. The guided meditation "A Walk in The Woods: Meditation for Adolescents," by Lou Irwin, LCSW, BCD, at the end of this section, provides an excellent exercise for adolescents to feel reconnected with the deceased. At the end of the meditation are questions for group discussion.

Activity 5: Important dates. Discuss with the group members how feelings may resurface during important times, such as anniversaries, birthdays, holidays, court dates, and other special occasions. Facilitate discussion about what can be helpful for them during these special times.

Closing Tasks

Facilitators need to discuss with the members that the group will be ending after 4 more sessions. Let them know that a ceremony will be held at the last session and plan with the members what type of food they would like and/or if they have any thoughts about things they can do in the group to celebrate the ending. Remind the group about confidentiality. Close the group with an ending ritual.

So Many Questions and "If Only..."

This time can be very confusing. You may be asking yourself and others many questions such as WHY did this happen, or why did it happen to them and not me? When a violent death occurs, it is normal for many questions to arise. Sometimes, people do not want to ask the questions because they are scared to let people really know what they are thinking about. Also, some of the questions may not have answers or ones that they want to hear. It is okay to have and ask these questions. Write down a couple of questions that have been on your mind.

_____

_____

_____

_____

_____

_____

_____

_____

_____

_____

_____

_____

_____

_____

*You may have found that as you asked these questions, **"If only"** thoughts started to surface. Thoughts that **"If only....** it would not have happened. **"If only....** I could have saved them." **"If only....**I would have....." While a lot of people have these thoughts, if you continue to blame yourself and feel guilty, it will start to take its toll. It may take a while to be at peace with yourself. However, other people can help you with this because they can reflect back to you that it was not your fault, you did the best you could, and/or there was nothing more you could have done.*

*Try to talk to people you trust about these thoughts of **"If only..."***

Staying Connected

When someone close dies, it is normal to want to stay connected. Some of the ways that people stay connected is by talking to the deceased, keeping their memory alive, and holding on to their belongings. This worksheet includes questions about your relationship with the person who has died. When you read the question, insert the name of the person who died. Take your time answering the questions.

1. Where do you think _____ is now? _____
_____

2. Do you ever communicate with_____ in anyway? If so, how? _____
_____
_____

3. Do you have any personal items of _____?

If so, what do you have and how does this make you feel? If not, do you want anything and what would it be? _____
_____
_____
_____

4. How often during the week do you think about _____ ? _____
_____

5. When you think about _____, what is it that you mostly think about? _____
_____
_____

6. Are there any special activities that you wish you could do to help you remember _____ in a special way?
_____
_____
_____

7. Is there anything that you want to ask _____ ? _____
_____
_____

8. Is there anything that you want to tell _____ about your life now? _____
_____
_____

9. What do you think _____ would say to you after you told them this?_____
_____
_____

A Walk in The Woods: Meditation for Adolescents

BY LOU IRWIN, L.C.S.W., B.C.D.

1. PURPOSE OF THIS MEDITATION:

This meditation, or guided imagery, is an example of a relaxation technique that many people of all ages find useful. This particular meditation is for adolescents who have experienced a great loss- the loss of someone close due to violence. Before using this meditation with survivors, readers need to make sure that it does not include obvious words that would "trigger" trauma responses. For example, if the violent death occurred in a wooded area, the mediation may need to be changed to a walk in the garden.

For those who have lost someone to violence, doing this meditation is one of the many things to be done to help the healing process. One advantage of this exercise is that you can do it whenever you choose, when you are by yourself or when you do not want to talk with someone else. It is a "tool," like a hammer and nails, that you do decide when to use – but it is not a replacement for talking with others.

2. BEGINNING:

To prepare for this meditation, first choose a place and position to sit in that makes you feel comfortable. Then, begin to pay attention to your breathing. It may help to close your eyes if you want to. Are you breathing fast? Is it shallow? Is it slow? Is it deep? Pay attention to how you feel when you suggest to yourself that you breathe more slowly and breathe more deeply. Do you find that hard to do? Do you find it easy? There is no right or wrong way to do this exercise. Whatever you experience is what you need to experience at this time and place. As you are ready, your breathing can slow down and deepen; you can breathe in more calmness and breathe out any troubling feelings or thoughts. Perhaps saying a word to yourself like "peace" or "calm" may help.

It may also help to count your breaths as you picture yourself going down steps. Take one breath as you count each step, starting with shallow breathes and gradually deepening your breathing as you count each step with each breath — 1, 2, 3, 4, 5...

Sometimes, as you are paying attention to your breathing, some troubling thought or feeling comes to mind. If this happens, try not to fight the feeling or thought. Instead, just be aware of it, maybe give it a name. Once you have named it, you may picture a cloud floating across the sky. Then, you can picture yourself putting the troubling thought or feeling on a cloud and letting it gently float away.

As the disturbing thought or feeling floats away, return back to your breathing -- breathing more and more deeply in and out.

3. WALK IN THE WOODS:

After you have gone down a series of steps, you find yourself on a path, with woods on both sides. You walk at an easy pace, taking in the sights and sounds and smells of the woods. Looking over to your right, you may see the sunlight filtering through the tree branches. You also feel the cool breeze blowing against your face, helping you feel relaxed and calm. In the branches of the trees, you can see and hear birds singing and calling to each other. You smell the rich earth around you. Each sight, sound, and smell fits your overall experience of the woods as a peaceful place.

Up ahead, you hear water of a small stream bubbling and flowing over rocks and pebbles. As you get nearer to the stream, you can see the multiple reflections on the water. The sunlit water seems to dance as it flows on its way. As you reach the bank of the stream, you see stones large enough to step on and cross the water. You step on each of these — one, two, three — and reach the other side.

Still hearing the soothing flow of the stream, you walk on ahead. On each side the woods continue. Looking ahead, you begin to see a clearing. As you get closer to this clearing, you see a meadow that is filled with flowers and tall grass. The wind blows the flowers and the grass back and forth in a beautiful dance. As you reach the edge of the meadow, you see a large rock that looks very comfortable for sitting. You sit on the rock and look out over the meadow. You feel at peace. Perhaps you close your eyes. As you are resting, you think good things about the person you lost to violence. Perhaps you even have a sensation that this person wants to communicate with you now. Then, an animal appears and you have the unusual experience that the person you lost is going to communicate to you through this animal. The animal stops and looks directly at you. In the eyes of the animal you experience the love and acceptance and connection that you used to feel with that person. You have all the time you need to talk to the person – to say things you have wanted to say and to hear things that they want to say to you. Somehow this setting and this animal can make it easier for you to say and hear the words that need to be said. You feel a range of emotions, but mainly you are aware of the great love and happiness that connects you and this person. Take as much time as you need to do all the talking that you need to do. Slowly speak from your heart and — hear their message. [Long pause]

After taking in what is needed at this time, your conversation will come to an end. But you know that you can return to this conversation whenever you need to talk to them. So, when you are ready, the animal jumps away and you open your eyes and see the beautiful meadow without any animals in sight. You may feel a lot of emotions, but you are most aware that the deep love of connection is underneath and within all other emotions you are feeling.

You stand up and begin to walk back to where you started. You take one last look at the meadow, then walk down the path to the stream. There at the stream, you step on the three stones again, and get on the other side. Then you walk again on the path noticing once more the sunlight, the birds and other animals and the breeze blowing through the trees.

When you reach the end of the path, you are aware of this meditation coming to an end. Begin to focus back on your breathing, in and out, in and out. You may picture those steps that helped you breathe more deeply as you were beginning to do this meditation. If you can see those steps, picture yourself walking up them as you count your breathes from five back to one, 5,4,3,2,1... When you reach the top step, gradually open your eyes and come back fully in the room where you have done this meditation. Take time to look around you and get accustomed again to being in this room. Know that you can bring with you into this room everything you experienced on your "walk in the woods."

4. REFLECTIVE QUESTIONS ABOUT YOUR MEDITATION:

What was this experience like for you?

What parts were the most relaxing and calming (you may want to do more of these next time)?

What helped you get through any troubling part?

Do you need to write about this experience in a journal or draw a picture about it?

Is there anyone you want to talk with about this experience?

Session Seven

Topics: Explore feelings of anger and revenge, teach anger management, provide education about specific issues

Opening Tasks

Briefly review group rules. Check in with group members to see how they are doing and how they are feeling. Asking about their feelings reinforces the previous group discussion about identifying feelings. Explain what will be addressed in this session. Ask if anyone brought a photograph or something special from the person who died and let them share it with the group. Let them know they only have 2 more sessions to bring something.

Activity 1: Explore feelings of anger and teach anger management. When discussing anger, facilitators need to help members articulate feelings of anger toward other people and systems. Anger management concepts and techniques such as triggers, recognizing body responses to anger, ways to stop acting, displaced anger, and ways to channel anger should be taught, depending on the needs of the group. There are many anger management workbooks that can assist the facilitators with this topic. In addition, there are many videos that can be helpful. For example the film, "Anger, Rage and You" (Robbins, 1996) uses a multicultural approach to address this topic. Prothrow-Stith (1987) developed and implemented a violence prevention curriculum for urban adolescents, which provides excellent activities to help teenagers with anger. The worksheet entitled "Anger," which is at the end of this section, also can be used as a tool to discuss anger management.

Activity 2: Explore feelings of revenge. Facilitators may want to reread the section on revenge in chapter 8 before facilitating the discussion about revenge. If members in the group have had someone die due to homicide, including vehicular homicide, the topic of revenge needs to be addressed. Members may have strong thoughts, feelings, and values about this topic.

Activity 3: Specific education. Depending upon the types of violent death and surrounding circumstances, different information may need to be discussed. For example, with accidental deaths, adolescents may want specific information about safety, such as fire safety, water safety, etc. and how they can get involved in preventative efforts; with homicidal deaths, adolescents may want to learn about the criminal justice system; and with suicidal deaths, adolescents may want more information about why people commit suicide and suicide prevention. For more information about suicide, facilitators may want to use the handouts about suicide in chapter 12.

Closing Tasks

Facilitators need to discuss with the members that the group will be ending after 3 more sessions. Confirm any plans for the celebration in the last session. Remind the group members about confidentiality. Close the group with an ending ritual.

Anger

Anger is a normal human emotion and feeling it is okay. However, when something like this happens the angry feelings can feel very intense. Sometimes angry feelings can be used to create positive changes. But, if you do not handle your angry feelings in constructive ways, these feelings may lead to behaviors that hurt you or others. One of the first steps to controlling your anger is to understand it better. Recognize your anger and learn ways to handle it.

**I FEEL ANGRY FOR THE FOLLOWING REASONS
(LIST SOME OF THE REASONS WHY YOU FEEL ANGRY):**

1. _____

2. _____

3. _____

WHEN I AM ANGRY MY BODY RESPONDS BY (CHECK ALL THAT APPLY):

❑ *sweating*   ❑ *headache*

❑ *tight fist*   ❑ *tight jaw and teeth clamped*

❑ *heart racing*   ❑ *list other ways*

_____

_____

_____

I HAVE NOTICED THAT I USUALLY FEEL ANGRY WHEN (COMPLETE THIS SENTENCE): _____

_____

WHO CAN YOU TALK WITH ABOUT YOUR ANGRY FEELINGS? _____

_____

TRY TO LIST AT LEAST FIVE THINGS THAT YOU CAN DO TO HELP YOU CONTROL YOUR ANGER:

1. _____

2. _____

3. _____

4. _____

5. _____

Session Eight

Topics: Identify supports, list coping techniques, discuss spirituality, examine family reactions and interactions, explore meaning in life

Opening Tasks

Very briefly review group rules. Check in with group members. Explain what will be addressed in this session. Ask if anyone brought a photograph or something special from the person who died and let them share it with the group. Let them know they only have 1 more session to bring something to share.

Activity 1: Identify supports. Discuss the importance of having supportive people in their lives and again ask them to identify supportive people. Ask members if they have been talking with these people about their thoughts and feelings about what has happened. If not, encourage them to identify one person with whom they will try to talk, perhaps by sharing some of what they have been doing in the group sessions.

Activity 2: Compile a list of coping techniques. As a group, have members brainstorm and list 25 things they can do to feel better when they are grieving, or to help "soften" the grief. Inform them that the facilitators will compile the group list and give each member a copy at the next session. It is recommended that this coping list be typed on colored paper or paper with special graphics on it so that it looks more important and official. The coping list will not have members' names on it so that confidentiality is protected.

Activity 3: Spirituality/Religion. If the topic of spirituality and/or God has not been previously discussed in another session or when a coping list was completed, facilitators should raise the issue of spirituality/religion, as it is one of the major influencing factors that often guides the youth's beliefs about afterlife and provides specific mourning rituals. Religion is often a source of help for bereaved adolescents, but not for all youth, as some may be angry with God or not believe in God (Balk, 1983). Facilitators need to make sure that such discussion about the role of religion can be honestly explored without disrespect or judgment from facilitators or other members. Appendix B provides a list of books that provide information about different religious and cultural practices after death. Group members should be encouraged to talk with someone in their family or someone on their list of supports about this issue.

Activity 4: Family reactions and interactions. Discuss with the group members that while they have expressed common grief and trauma reactions, they have also expressed different ways of coping. It is often helpful for adolescents to talk about how the violent death has affected their family and their interactions with different family members. Following are some discussion questions that facilitators may use when discussing family reactions and interactions.

1. Has anyone noticed how other family members have acted differently since the death?
2. Have things changed in any way with your family since the death? How?
3. Is there any family member whom you worry about since the death? If so, why?
4. Have you noticed any changes in your relationships with any family members?
5. Is there anything you wish you could change for your family?
6. Is there anything you would like to change regarding your relationships with your family?

Activity 5: Explore sense of meaning in one's life. This topic of meaning may have already emerged when discussing spirituality. As discussed in chapter 4, it is extremely important that adolescents have a sense of meaning in life. The worksheet at the end of this section entitled "Everyday Life and Meaning" may be used to address this issue. If adolescents are not able to identify people or things that they care about, this may be an indication that further intervention is needed.

Closing Tasks

Facilitators need to discuss with the members that the group will be ending after 2 more sessions and allow them time to discuss their thoughts and feelings about this. Remind the group members about confidentiality and close with an ending ritual.

Every Day Life and Meaning

Coping with what has happened and grieving for those who died may take a very long time. Some would say, "It will take a lifetime." This may be true, but over time, with help from others — family, relatives, friends, teachers, neighbors, religious leaders, a doctor or counselor — you can start to feel better.

At some point, re-engaging in your every day life is important. Try to start doing things you used to do before the death. Yes, you may feel and think differently about a lot of things, but participating in the everyday activities of life can really help.

While finding the "meaning" in one's life is sometimes a life-long journey, it is important during this time to clarify the things in your life that are important to you. This may be honoring the person who died, holding on to memories of the person who died, having a strong spiritual base, strengthening the relationships in your life, planning for your future, excelling in school, participating in sports, or appreciating nature.

IN THE CIRCLE BELOW, WRITE DOWN ALL THE THINGS THAT YOU CARE ABOUT AND REMEMBER THESE AS YOU GO ABOUT YOUR EVERYDAY LIFE:

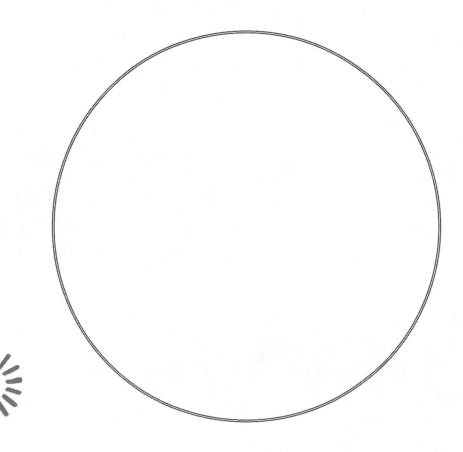

Session Nine

Topics: Review progress of goals, administer posttest, future goals

Opening Tasks

Very briefly review group rules. Check in with group members. Explain what will be addressed in this session. Ask if anyone brought a photograph or something special from the person who died and let them share it with the group.

Give group members a copy of the coping list they compiled in session 8. Encourage members to keep this in a place where they will not lose it and can often look at it. Also, members may want to give this list to other people they know who are grieving and/or post it at their school.

Finalize plans for the last session.

Activity 1: Review of goals. On each "Review of Group Goals" handout which is included at the end of this section, write each member's name and the personal goals that they listed on the first goal sheet from session 3. Ask members to review and rank the progress toward the group goals and any individual goals listed (using a 10-point scale with 0 being no progress and 10 being goal met).

Activity 2: Administer the standardized posttest assessment scale. This should be the same scale that was administered in session 2. See section on evaluation in chapter 14.

Activity 3: Future goals. Getting adolescents, especially youth who have had someone close die, to think about their future goals and dreams is very important. Sometimes youth who have been traumatized may have a difficult time with this. On a sheet of paper, have members express (in writing or by drawing) what their goals or dreams are for their future. On the back of the sheet, have them write at least three things that will help them reach these goals. Encourage them to iden-tify short-term goals that they can accomplish that will contribute to the success of reaching more long-term goals. Another activity for this topic may include making collages about things they want for their future. Again, have them list 3 things they need to do to in the immediate future to reach these goals.

Activity 4: Allow time during this session for members to finish any past activities that they did not have time to complete or to work in a journal or individual workbook that may have been given to them at the beginning of the group.

Closing Tasks

Discuss feelings about the group ending. Facilitators may need to model expressing feelings about ending (see chapter 5, Separation–Termination). Remind the group members about confidentiality and close with an ending ritual.

Review of Group Goals

Name: _____   Date: _____

THESE GOALS WERE SET AT THE BEGINNING OF GROUP. ON THE SCALES, PLEASE CIRCLE
A NUMBER INDICATING THE AMOUNT OF PROGRESS FOR EACH GOAL.

1 MEANS THAT THE GOAL WAS NOT MET AT ALL AND 10 MEANS THE GOAL WAS MET.

1. I learned more about grief and trauma reactions.

    1   2   3   4   5   6   7   8   9   10
    Did not learn > Learned a lot

2. I expressed my thoughts and feelings about what has happened.

    1   2   3   4   5   6   7   8   9   10
    Did not express myself > Expressed myself a lot

The personal goals you set for yourself during the third meeting are written below.
Please rank the progress of each goal using the ten-point scale.

1. _____
    1   2   3   4   5   6   7   8   9   10
    Did not meet my goal > Goal met

2. _____
    1   2   3   4   5   6   7   8   9   10
    Did not meet my goal > Goal met

Has this group been helpful for you? If yes, how? If no, why not?

_____

_____

_____

_____

_____

Session Ten

Topics: Recognize progress, provide recognition, terminate

Opening Tasks

Very briefly review group rules. Check in with group members. Explain what will be addressed in this session. Set up and serve refreshments. This should include food and drink that the members requested in session 6 and any other special request such as music. Allow some time for informal interaction and enjoyment.

Activity 1: Progress and recognition. Facilitators need to create a certificate of completion for each group member. Official certificates can be purchased at any office or school supply store. Certificates should be presented in the group to each youth. As they are being distributed, facilitators should provide feedback regarding the progress that each member made in the 10-week group. Group members are encouraged to add positive statements. Each member is then asked to state something they learned from the group experience and/or something about the group that has been helpful for them. They may include things they like about the group and things they did not like.

Activity 2: Termination. Allow group members to express their feelings about the group ending, including ambivalent feelings that they may have (see chapter 5, Separation–Termination).

Closing Tasks

Let members know that facilitators will be contacting their parent or guardian about the group ending. Although details of the group will not be shared, facilitators may make further recommendations if they feel members may need additional counseling. Also, inform all members that there may be other times in their life that they decide to participate in a group or need to get additional support for coping.

If workbooks or journals were used, group members are given these to keep.

Ending Ritual

Let the group members choose if they want to end in the same way or if they want to end in a different way for the last group.

Facilitators Meeting

Facilitators should schedule one additional meeting at the same time and location especially if the group was community-based. This allows the facilitators to discuss the process of the group and each individual member. Ideally, a follow-up meeting with all parents and guardians needs to occur, but this may not be possible. If members scored high on the standardized posttraumatic or traumatic grief posttest, indicated low attainment on the goals, and/or continued to appear highly distressed or have low functioning levels, further recommendations need to be made (individual or family therapy and/or pharmacology). Also, it is a good idea to give the parent/guardian information about community resources, should they need help in the future, and to explain that at different developmental stages the youth may revisit some of his or her initial violent death-related reactions and will need extra support. For example, when an adolescent graduates from high school, he or she may feel the profound loss of his or her loved one not being there. Parents should be made aware of these potentially difficult times (including holidays and anniversary dates) and encouraged to offer additional support and understanding during these times.

Appendix A

Resource Organizations for Crisis Intervention and Information About Violent Death

American Red Cross

Provides training in mental health crisis response. In times of disasters they provide emergency disaster needs, such as shelter, food, health and mental health services, blood, information to survivors and victims, and care to relief workers. Web site has information in Spanish and English. (202) 303–4498 or http://www.redcross.org/.

International Critical Incident Stress Foundation, Inc.

Provides a variety of training related to critical incident stress management. Certifications programs are offered as well. Has a national network of trained responders. (410) 750–9600, Emergency (410) 313–2473, or http://www.icisf.org.

National Organization for Victims Assistance (NOVA)

Provides basic and advanced crisis response training. NOVA also promotes rights and services for crime victims. They also have a national advocacy credentialing program. Provides information and referral for victims of crime and disasters. (800) TRY-NOVA, (202) 232–6682, or http:// www.try-nova.org.

National Center for Children Exposed to Violence

School Crisis Prevention and Response Initiative provides planning, training, and technical assistance for addressing problems arising from crises. (877) 49-NCCEV or http://www.nccev.org.

U.S. Department of Education

This department works in conjunction with other federal departments and agencies (such as Safe and Drug Free Schools and the Centers for Disease Control and Prevention) to provide information about crisis management. A specific Web site is available for school leaders, which has information on guides for crisis planning, dealing with trauma in schools, preparing for terrorist attacks, and more. http://www.ed.gov/emergencyplan/.

Additional National Resource Organizations that Provide Information Regarding Adolescents After Violent Death

AboutOurKids.org

The New York University Child Study Center sponsors AboutOurKids.org. The Web site http://www.aboutourkids.org provides information for parents, educators, and mental health professionals about a range of issues regarding children and adolescents. The Web site has a quick search feature that makes it easy to find information about grief and trauma.

A Gift From Within

This international nonprofit organization is for survivors of trauma and victimization who suffer from posttraumatic stress and for those who care for traumatized people. The Web site http://www.giftfromwithin.org provides a wealth of information, including articles about auto accidents, national tragedies, grief, and school disasters. (207) 236–8858.

American Association of Sociology (AAS)

Provides information about suicide, support groups, and research regarding suicide. The mission of the AAS is to understand and prevent suicide. (202) 237–2280 or http://www.Suicidology. org.

MADD (Mothers Against Drunk Driving)

MADD's mission is to stop drunk driving and provide support to victims. There are more than 600 chapters nationwide. (800) GET-MADD or http://www.madd.org.

National Center for Grieving Children and Families (Dougy Center for Grieving Children)

Provides training and workshops. Books for adults, schools, children, adolescents, and mental health professionals can be purchased at their online resource center. (503) 775–5683 or http://www.grievingchild.org.

National Center for Posttraumatic Stress Disorder (NCPTSD)

The NCPTSD Web site has excellent information about children, adolescents, and adults and trauma, disasters, war, community violence, motor vehicle accidents, anniversary reactions, ethnocultural differences, media, and so on. The information sheets are useful to give to parents, teachers, and adolescents who want more information. At this site you also can access the PILOTS database, which contains more than 20,000 abstracts from various disciplines about traumatic stress. (802) 296–6300 or http://www.ncptsd.org/.

National Center for Victims of Crime (NCVC)

NCVC launched The Teen Victim Project, which specifically addresses issues regarding adolescent victimization. Information about the Teen Victim Project can be found at http://www.ncvc.org/tvp/. (Information is available in English or Spanish.) (202) 467–8700 or helpline (800) FYI-CALL.

National Organization of Parents of Murdered Children (POMC)

This national organization has local chapters to offer support for parents and friends who have had loved ones die by violence. POMC provides support, education, advocacy, and awareness. (888) 818–POMC or http://www.pomc.org.

National Youth Violence Prevention Resource Center (NYVPRC)

Provides information and resources regarding youth violence and suicide and about effective strategies to control and prevent such violence. Specific information for parents, teens, and health care professionals is provided. The center, which is a collaboration between the Centers for Disease Control and Prevention and other federal agencies, includes a bilingual (Spanish/English) toll-free telephone information line (886) SAFEYOUTH or (886) 968–8484 or http://www.safeyouth.org.

Students Against Destructive Behaviors (founded as Students Against Drunk Driving)

This is a nationwide youth leadership program with local chapters. It focuses on educating young people to make positive decisions to avoid destructive behaviors, and provides programs and education aimed at preventing underage drinking, drug use, impaired driving, and other destructive behaviors. (877) SADD-INC or http://www.SADD.com.

Suicide Prevention Advocacy Network

This network provides information on suicide prevention and lists several resources. (770) 998–8819 or http://www.spanusa.org.

The Compassionate Friends (TCF)

The Compassionate Friends is a national, nonprofit support organization with local chapters to assist grieving families. To find a local chapter call (877) 696–0010. Also, the Web site provides TCF brochures about a range of grief-related topics, which are in English and Spanish. http://www.compassionatefriends.org.

The National Institute for Trauma and Loss in Children (TLC)

TLC provides education, training, and resource materials to schools, parents, and mental health professionals to help children, parents, and schools traumatized by violence. Trauma and Loss certification programs and books and videos are available. Toll-free at (877) 306–5256 or http://www.tlcinst.org.

Office for Victims of Crime, U.S. Department of Justice

The Office for Victims of Crime provides funding and training for victims of crime service providers and sponsors the National Crime Victim Rights Week. The Web site lists numerous OVC publications about victims issues. (202) 370–5983 or http://www.ojp.usdoj.gov/ovc/.

Violence and Injury Prevention (VIP) Web site

This Web site provides articles, resources, stories, and other links concerned with suicide, homicide, and homicide-suicide. http://www.fmhi.usf.edu/amh/homicide-suicide/.

Violent Dying Bereavement Society

This Society provides training, information, consultation, research, and a network for service providers who work with people after violent death. (206) 233–6398 or http://www.vdbs.org.

Appendix B
Additional Resources Regarding Culture, Bereavement, and Trauma

Brice, C. (1999). *Lead me home: An African American guide through the grief journey*. New York: Avon Books. Excellent source of inspiration for bereaved African-American adults and adolescents. Includes one- to two-page meditations and exercises for healing.

Grollman, E. A. (Ed.). (1995). *Bereaved children and teens: A support guide for parents and professionals*. Boston, MA: Beacon Press. Includes cultural, philosophical, and religious perspectives on death and children. Specific information regarding African-American children. Protestant, Catholic, and Jewish perspectives discussed.

Irish, D. P., Lundquist, K. F., & Nelson, V. J. (Eds.). (1993). *Ethnic variations in dying, death, and grief: Diversity in universality*. Washington, DC: Taylor & Francis. Includes information about funeral and mourning customs of African Americans, Mexican Americans, Hmongs, Native Americans, and Judaism, Buddhism, Islam, Quakerism, and Unitarianism.

Parkes, C. M., Laungani, P., Young, B., & Young, B. (Eds.). (1997). *Death and bereavement across cultures*. New York: Routledge. Includes cultural bereavement information about Hinduism, Tibetan Buddhism, Judaism, Christianity, and Islam.

Nader, K., Dubrow, N., & Stamm, B. H. (Eds.) (1999). *Honoring differences: Cultural issues in the treatment of trauma and loss*. Philadelphia: Brunner/Mazel. Discusses cultural responses of African Americans, Native North Americans, Mexican Americans, Asian Americans, and in Africa, Israel, former Yugoslavia, and Palestine, to trauma and loss.

Walsh, F., & McGoldrick, M. (1995). *Living beyond loss: Death in the family*. New York: W.W. Norton. Includes information regarding mourning practices of Irish families, Hindu Indian families, African American families, Puerto Rican families, Jewish families, and Chinese families.

Workbooks to Use with Adolescents After Violent Death

Deaton, W., & Johnson, K. (1998). *I saw it happen*. Alameda, CA: Hunter House. While this book is designed for children age 8 to 12, it is an excellent book to use with adolescents who have witnessed violence. The book includes both writing and drawing activities and is designed to help children who are experiencing trauma due to witnessing violence. To order, contact Hunter House at (800) 266–5592 or http://www.hunterhouse.com.

Heegaard, M. (1992). *When something terrible happens: Children can learn to cope*. Minneapolis, MN: Woodland Press. This book is generally for elementary aged children, but it has been used with adolescents, especially with teenagers who like to draw. This book may be ordered at Centering Corporation at (402) 553–1200 or http://www.centering.org.

Salloum, A. (1998). *Reactions: A workbook to help young people who are experiencing trauma and grief*. Omaha, NE: Centering Corporation. This book discusses both grief and trauma reactions that may occur after someone close is murdered. It offers a combination of interactive activities such as checking boxes (for youth who don't like to write), space for drawing, and sentences and questions for short answer responses. Contact Centering Corporation at (402) 553–1200 or http://www.centering.org to obtain a copy.

Traisman, E. (1992). *Fire in my heart, ice in my veins*. Omaha, NE: Centering Corporation. This book offers an excellent format for journaling. Because it is long, it may not be finished during the time-limited group, but it may be given to the adolescent to finish on his or her own. Contact Centering Corporation at (402) 553–1200 or http://www.centering.org to obtain a copy.

References

American Psychiatric Association (2003). *Psychiatric effects of media violence.* APA online public information. Retrieved September 6, 2003, from http://www. psych.org/_info/media _violence.cfm

Arnett, J. J. (1999). Adolescent storm and stress, reconsidered. *American Psychologist, 54,* 317–326.

Baker, J. E., Sedney, M. A., & Gross, E. (1992). Psychological tasks for bereaved children. *American Journal of Orthopsychiatry, 62,* 105–116.

Balk, D. (1983). Effects of sibling death on teenagers. *Journal of School Health, 53,* 14–18.

Balk, D. E. (1990). The self-concepts of bereaved adolescents: Sibling death and its aftermath. *Journal of Adolescent Research, 5,* 112–132.

Bard, M., Arnone, H. C., & Nemiroff, D. (1986). Contextual influences on the post-traumatic stress adaptation of homicide survivor-victims. In C. R. Figley (Ed.), *Trauma and its wake. Volume II: Traumatic stress theory, research and intervention* (pp. 292–304). New York: Brunner/Mazel.

Berman, S. L., Kurtines, W. M., Silverman, W. K., & Serafini, L. T. (1996). The impact of exposure to crime and violence on urban youth. *American Journal of Orthopsychiatry, 66,* 329–335.

Black, D. (1984). Sundered families: The effects of loss of a parent. *Adoption and Fostering, 8,* 38–43.

Brent, D. A., Perper, J. A., Moritz, G., Liotus, L., Richardson, D., Canobbio, R., Schweers, J., & Roth, C. (1994). Posttraumatic stress disorder in peers of adolescent suicide victims: Predisposing factors and phenomenology. *Journal of the American Academy of Child and Adolescent Psychiatry, 34,* 209–215.

Bronfenbrenner, U. (1989). Ecological systems theory. *Annals of Child Development, 6,* 187–249.

Carlson, E. (1997). *Trauma assessment: A clinician's guide.* New York: Guilford Press.

Centers for Disease Control and Prevention, National Center for Injury Prevention and Control. 10 Leading Causes of Death, US, 1999–2000, Age Group 10–20. Retrieved August 27, 2003, from *http://webapp.cdc.gov/cgi-bin/broker.exe*

Chachkes, E., & Jennings, R. (1994). Latino communities: Coping with death. In B.O. Dane & C. Levin (Eds.), AIDS and the new orphans: Coping with death (pp. 77–99). Westport, CT: Auburn House.

Christ, G. H. (2000). Impact of development on children's mourning. *Cancer Practice, 8,* 72–81.

Clark, D. C., Pynoos, R. S., & Goebel, A. E. (1996). Mechanisms and processes of adolescent bereavement. In R. Hoggerty, L. Sherrad, N. Garmezy, & M. Rutter (Eds.), *Stress, risk and resilience: Children and adolescents* (pp. 100–146). New York: Cambridge University Press.

Clark, T. (2003, Summer). Media matters: Victims' guide to the media helps victims of trauma deal with media questions. *Traumatic Stress Points, 17,* (3).

Cohen, J. A. (1998). Summary of the practice parameters for the assessment and treatment of children and adolescents with posttraumatic stress disorder. *Journal of the American Academy of Child and Adolescent Psychiatry, 37,* 997–1001.

Cohen, J. A., Mannarino, A. P., Greenberg, T., Padlo, S., & Shipley, C. (2002). Childhood traumatic grief: Concepts and controversies. *Trauma, Violence and Abuse, 4,* 307–327.

Corr, C. A. (1995). Entering into adolescent understanding of death. In E. A. Grollman (Ed.), *Bereaved children and teens: A support guide for parents and professionals*. Boston: Beacon Press.

Corr, C., Nabe, C. N., & Corr, D. M. (1997). *Death and dying, life and living* (2nd ed.). Pacific Grove, CA: Brooks/Cole Publishing Co.

Costello, J. E., Erkanli, A., Fairbank, J. A., & Angold, A. (2002). The prevalence of potentially traumatic events in childhood and adolescence. *Journal of Traumatic Stress, 15*, 99–112.

Crenshaw, D. A. (1996). *Bereavement: Counseling the grieving throughout the life cycle*. New York: Crossroad Publishing.

Deaton, W., & Johnson, K. (1998). *I saw it happen*. Alameda, CA: Hunter House.

Diagnostic and Statistical Manual of Mental Disorders, Fourth Edition, Text Revision. (2000). Washington, DC, American Psychiatric Association.

Duncan, D. F. (1996). Growing up under the gun: Children and adolescent coping with violent neighborhoods. *Journal of Primary Prevention, 16*, 343–356.

Eisenberg, N., Fabes, R. A., & Guthrie, I. K. (1997). *Coping with stress: The roles of regulation and development*. In S. A. Wolchik & I. N. Sandler (Eds.), *Handbook of children's coping: Linking theory and intervention* (pp. 41–70). New York: Plenum Press.

Eth, S., & Pynoos, R. S. (1994). Children who witness the homicide of a parent. *Psychiatry, 57*, 287–306.

Fitzpatrick, K. M., & Boldizar, J. P. (1993). The prevalence and consequences of exposure to violence among African-American youth. *Journal of the American Academy of Child and Adolescent Psychiatry, 32*, 424–430.

Frantuzzo, J. W., & Mohr, W. K. (1999). Prevalence and effects of child exposure to domestic violence. *The Future of Children, 9*. Los Altos, CA: The David and Lucile Packard Foundation.

Freeman, L. N., Shaffer, D., & Smith, H. (1996). Neglected victims of homicide: The needs of young siblings of murder victims. *American Journal of Orthopsychiatry, 66*, 337–345.

Freid, V. M., Prager, K., MacKay, A. P., & Xia, H. (2003). Chartbook on trends in the health of Americans. Health, United States, 2003. Hyattsville, MD: National Center for Health Statistics.

Garbarino, J. (1999). *Lost boys: Why our sons turn violent and how we can save them*. New York: Free Press.

Garbarino, J., Dubrow, N., Kostelny, K., & Pardo, C. (1992). *Children in danger: Coping with the consequences of community violence*. San Francisco: Jossey-Bass Publishers.

Garbarino, J., Kostelny, K., & Dubrow, N. (1991). What children can tell us about living in danger. *American Psychologist, 46*, 376–383.

Garcia-Preto, N. (1991). Mourning in different cultures: Puerto Rican Families. In F. Walsh & M. Goldrick (Eds.), *Living Beyond Loss: Death in the Family* (pp. 176–206). New York: W.W. Norton.

Giaconia, R. M., Reinherz, H. Z., Silverman, A., Pakiz, B., Frost, A., & Cohen, E. (1995). Traumas and posttraumatic stress disorder in a community population of older adolescents. *Journal of the American Academy of Child and Adolescent Psychiatry, 34*, 1369–1380.

Gibbs, J. T. (2001). African-American adolescents. In J. T Gibbs & L. N. Huang (Eds.), *Children of color: Psychological interventions with culturally diverse youth* (pp. 171–214). San Francisco: Jossey-Bass.

Goenjian, A. K., Karayan, I., Pynoos, R. S., Minassian, D., Najarian, L. M., Steinberg, A. M., & Fairbanks, L. A. (1997). Outcome of psychotherapy among early adolescents after trauma. *American Journal of Psychiatry, 154*, 536–542.

Grabowski, J., & Frantz, T. T. (1993). *Latinos and Anglos: Cultural experiences of grief intensity*. Omega, 26, 273–285.

Grollman, E. A. (1995). *Bereaved children and teens: A support guide for parents and professionals*. Boston: Beacon Press.

Hamblen, J. (2003). PTSD in children and adolescents. National Center for PTSD, Department of Veteran Affairs. Retrieved August 28, 2003, from http://www.ncptsd.org/facts/specifics/fs_children.

Hardwick, P. J., & Rowton-Lee, M. A. (1996). Adolescent homicide: towards assessment of risk. *Journal of Adolescence, 19,* 263–274.

Harris, E. S. (1991). Adolescent bereavement following the death of a parent: An exploratory study. *Child Psychiatry and Human Development, 21,* 267–281.

Heegaard, M. (1992). *When something terrible happens: children can learn to cope.* Minneapolis: MN: Woodland Press.

Hickey, L. O. (1993). Death of a counselor: A bereavement group for junior high school students. In N. Webb (Ed.), *Helping bereaved children: A handbook for practitioners* (pp. 239–266). New York: Guilford Press.

Hines, P. M. (1991). Death and African-American culture. In F. Walsh & M. McGoldrick (Eds.), *Living beyond loss: Death in the family* (pp. 186–194). New York: W.W. Norton.

Hogan, N., & DeSantis, L. (1992). Adolescent sibling bereavement: An ongoing attachment. *Qualitative Health Research, 2,* 159–177.

Hogan, N., & DeSantis, L. (1994). Things that help and hinder adolescent sibling bereavement. *Western Journal of Nursing Research, 16,* 132–153.

Horowitz, M., Siegel, B., Holen, A., Bonanno, G. A., Milbrath, C., & Stinson, C. (1997). Diagnostic Criteria for Complicated Grief Disorder. *American Journal of Psychiatry, 154,* 904–910.

Horowitz, M. J., Marmar, C., Weiss, D. S., DeWitt, K., & Rosenbaum, R. (1984). Brief psychotherapy of bereavement reactions. *Archives of General Psychiatry, 41,* 438–448.

Hovey, J. D., & King, C. A. (1996). Acculturative stress, depression, and suicidal ideation among immigrants and second-generation Latino adolescents. *Journal of the American Academy of Child and Adolescent Psychiatry, 35,* 1183–1192.

Jacobs, S., Mazure, C., & Prigerson, H. (2000). Diagnostic criteria for traumatic grief. *Death Studies, 24,* 185–199.

Johnson-Moore, P., & Phillips, L. (1994). Black American communities: Coping with death. In B. O. Dane and C. Levin (Eds.), *AIDS and the new orphans: Coping with death* (pp. 101–120). Westport, CT: Auburn House.

Kagawa-Singer, M. (1998). Introduction: Death rituals and mourning: A multicultural perspective. *Oncology Nursing Society, 25,* 1751–1756.

King, K. A. (1999). Fifteen prevalent myths concerning adolescent suicide. *Journal of School Health, 69,* 159–161.

King, K. A., Price, J. H., Telljohann, S. K., & Wahl, J. (1999). High school health teachers' perceived self-efficacy in identifying students at risk for suicide. *Journal of School Health, 69,* 202–207.

Kliewer, W., Lepore, S. J., Oskin, D., & Johnson, P. D. (1998). The role of social and cognitive process in children's adjustment to community violence. *Journal of Consulting and Clinical Psychology, 66,* 199–209.

Knight, G. P., & Hill, N. E. (1998). Measurement equivalence in research involving minority adolescents. In V. C. McLoyd & L. Steinberg (Eds.), *Studying minority adolescents: Conceptual, methodological, and theoretical issues* (pp. 183–210). Mahwah, NJ: Lawrence Erlbaum Associates.

Lazarus, R. S., & Folkman, S. (1984). *Stress, appraisal and coping.* New York: Springer Publishing.

Lee, W. (1995) Behind smiles and laughter: African-American children's issues about bereavement. In E. A. Grollman (Ed.), *Bereaved children and teens: A support guide for parents and professionals* (pp. 93–112). Boston: Beacon Press.

Levy, A. J., & Wall, J. C. (2000). Children who have witnessed community homicide: Incorporating risk and resilience in clinical work. *Families in Society, 81,* 402–411.

Lovrin, M. L. (1999). Parental murder and suicide: Post-traumatic stress disorder in children. *Journal of Child and Adolescent Psychiatric Nursing, 12,* 110–117.

March, J. S., Amaya-Jackson, L., Murry, M. C., & Schulte, A. (1998). Cognitive-behavioral psychotherapy for children and adolescents with posttraumatic stress disorder after a single-incident stressor. *Journal of Child and Adolescent Psychotherapy, 37,* 585–593.

McCann, I., & Pearlman, L. (1990). Vicarious traumatization: A framework for understanding the psychological effects of working with victims. *Journal of Traumatic Stress, 3,* 131–149.

McGoldrick, M., Almeida, R., Moore Hines, P., Garcia-Preto, N., Rosen, E., & Lee, E. (1991). Mourning in different cultures. In F. Walsh & M. McGoldrick (Eds.), *Living beyond loss: Death in the family* (pp. 176–206). New York: W.W. Norton.

McNeil, J. S. (1997). Bereavement and loss. In *Encyclopedia of social work (19th ed.)* (pp. 284–291). Washington, DC: National Association of Social Workers.

Meshot, C. M., & Leitner, L. M. (1993). Adolescent mourning and parental death. *Omega, 26,* 287–293.

Morin, S. M., & Welsh, L. A (1996). Adolescents' perceptions and experiences of death and grieving. *Adolescence, 31,* 585–596.

Munet-Vilaró, F. (1998). Grieving and death rituals of Latinos. *Oncology Nursing Forum, 25,* 1761–1763.

Murphy, S. A., Braun, T., Tillery, L., Cain, K. C., Johnson, C. L., & Beaton, R. (1999). PTSD among bereaved parents following the violent death of their 12- to 28-year-old children: A longitudinal prospective analysis. *Journal of Traumatic Stress, 12,* 273–292.

Nader, K. (1997). Assessing traumatic experiences in children. In J. P. Wilson & T. M. Keane (Eds.), *Assessing Psychological Trauma and PTSD* (pp. 291–348). New York: Guilford Press.

Nader, K., Pynoos, R. S., Fairbanks, L. A., & Frederick, C. J. (1990). Children's PTSD reactions one year after a sniper attack at their school. *American Journal of Psychiatry, 147,* 1526–1530.

National Center for Posttraumatic Stress Disorder. (n.d.). What is posttraumatic stress disorder: A national center for PTSD fact sheet. Retrieved August 8, 2003, from *http://www.ncptsd.org/facts/general/fs*

National Vital Statistics Report (2000, July 24). 48, 11.

Nolen-Hoeksema, S. (1992). Children coping with uncontrollable stressors. *Applied and Preventative Psychology, 1,* 183–189.

Northen, H., & Kurland, R. (2001). *Social Work with Groups (3rd ed.).* New York: Columbia University Press.

Oltjenbruns, K. A. (1998). Ethnicity and the grief response: Mexican-American vs. Anglo American College students. *Death Studies, 22,* 141–155.

Oltjenbruns, K. A. (1991). Positive outcomes of adolescents' experience with grief. *Journal of Adolescent Research, 6,* 43–53.

Osofsky, J. D., Wewers, S., Hann, D. M., & Fick, A. C. (1993). Chronic community violence: What is happening to our children? *Psychiatry, 56,* 36–45.

Overstreet, S., Dempsey, M., Graham, D., & Moely, B. (1999). Availability of family support as a moderator of exposure to community violence. *Journal of Clinical Child Psychology, 28,* 151–159.

Perry, H. L. (1993) Mourning and Funeral Customs of African Americans. In D. P. Irish, K.F. Lundquist, & V. J. Nelson (Eds.), *Ethnic variations in dying, death, and grief: diversity in universality* (pp. 51–65). Washington, DC: Taylor & Francis.

Petersen, A. C., & Leffert, N. (1995). What is so special about adolescence? In M. Rutter (Ed.), *Psychological disturbances in young people: Challenges for prevention* (pp. 3–36). New York: Cambridge University Press.

Pfeffer, C., Jiang, H., Kakuma, T., Hwang, J., & Metsch, M. (2002). Group intervention for children bereaved by the suicide of a relative. *Journal of the American Academy of Child and Adolescent Psychiatry, 41,* 805–514.

Pfefferbaum, B., Call, J. A., & Sconzo, G. M. (1999). Mental health services for children in the first two years after the 1995 Oklahoma City terrorist bombing. *Psychiatric Services, 50,* 956–958.

Pfefferbaum, B., Nixon, S. J., Tucker, P., Tivis, R., Moore, V., Gurwitch, R. H., et al. (1999). Posttraumatic stress responses in bereaved children after the Oklahoma City bombing. *Journal of the American Academy of Child and Adolescent Psychiatry, 38,* 1372–1383.

Pfefferbaum, B., Seale, T. W., McDonald, N. B., Brant, E. N., Rainwater, S. M., Maynard, B. T.,

Meierhoefer, B., & Peteryne, D. M. (2000). Posttraumatic stress two years after the Oklahoma City bombing in youths geographically distant for the explosion. *Psychiatry, 63,* 358–370.

Podell, C. (1989). Adolescent mourning: The sudden death of a peer. *Clinical Social Work, 17,* 64–78.

Prothrow-Stith, D. (1987). *Violence prevention curriculum for adolescents.* Newton, MA: Education Development Center.

Pynoos, R. S., & Eth, S. (1984). The child as witness to homicide. *Journal of Social Issues, 40,* 87–108.

Pynoos, R. S., Frederick, C., Nader, K., Arroyo, W., Steinberg, A., Eth, S., et al. (1987). Life threat and post-traumatic stress in school-age children. *Archives of General Psychiatry, 44,* 1057–1063.

Pynoos, R., & Nader, K. (1988). Psychological first aid and treatment approach to children exposed to community violence: Research implications. *Journal of Traumatic Stress, 4,* 445–473.

Pynoos, R. S., & Nader, K. (1990). Children's exposure to violence and traumatic death. *Psychiatric Annals, 20,* 334–344.

Ramirez, O. (2001). Mexican-American children and adolescents. In J. T Gibbs & L. N. Huang (Eds.), Children of color: *Psychological interventions with culturally diverse youth* (pp. 215–239). San Francisco: Jossey-Bass.

Rando, T. A. (1992–93). The increasing prevalence of complicated mourning: The onslaught is just the beginning. *Omega, 26,* 43–59.

Rando, T. A. (1993). *Treatment of complicated mourning.* Champaign, IL: Research Press.

Raphael, B., & Martinek, N. (1997). Assessing traumatic bereavement and posttraumatic stress disorder. In J. P. Wilson & T. M. Keane (Eds.), *Assessing psychological trauma and PTSD* (pp. 373–395). New York: Guilford Press.

Richters, J. E., & Martinez, P. (1993). The NIMH community violence project: I. Children as victims of and witnesses to violence. *Psychiatry, 56,* 7–21.

Ringler, L. L., & Hayden, D. C. (2000). Adolescent bereavement and social supports: Peer loss compared to other losses. *Journal of Adolescent Research, 15,* 209–229.

Robbins, J. (1996). *Anger, rage and you.* Pleasantville, NY: Sunburst Communications, Inc.

Romero, A. J., & Roberts, R. E. (2003). Stress within a bicultural context for adolescents of Mexican descent. *Cultural Diversity and Ethnic Minority Psychology, 9,* 171–184.

Rynearson, E. K. (2001). *Retelling violent death.* Philadelphia: Brunner-Routledge.

Rynearson, E. K., Favell, J. L., Belloumini, V., Gold, R., & Prigerson, H. (2002). Bereavement intervention with incarcerated youths. *Journal of the Academy of Child and Adolescent Psychiatry, 41,* 893–894.

Saleebey, D. (Ed.). (1997). *The strength perspective in social work practice (2nd ed.).* White Plains, NY: Longman Publishing Group.

Salloum, A. (1998). *Reactions: A workbook to help young people who are experiencing trauma and grief.* Omaha, NE: Centering Corporation.

Salloum, A. (2002). Homicide: Helping children in the aftermath. National Center for PTSD *Clinical Quarterly, 11,* 44–48.

Salloum, A., Avery, L., & McClain, R. P. (2001). Group psychotherapy for adolescent survivors of homicide victims: A pilot study. *Journal of the American Academy of Child and Adolescent Psychiatry, 40,* 1261–1267.

Salloum, A., & Vincent, N. J. (1999). Community-based groups for inner city adolescent survivors of homicide victims. *Journal of Child and Adolescent Group Therapy, 9,* 27–45.

Saltzman, W. R., Pynoos, R. S., Layne, C. M., Steinberg, A. M., & Aisenberg, E. (2001). Trauma- and grief-focused intervention for adolescents exposed to community violence: Results of a school-based screening and group treatment protocol. *Group Dynamics: Theory, Research and Practice, 5,* 291–303.

Schachter, S. (1991). Adolescent experience with the death of a peer. *Omega, 24,* 1–11.

Schilling, R. F., Koh, N., Abramovitz, R., & Gilbert, L. (1992). Bereavement groups for inner city children. *Research on Social Work Practice, 2* (3), 405–419.

Shore, R. (2003). *KIDS COUNT indicator brief: Reducing the teen death rate.* The Annie E. Casey Foundation. http://www.aecf.org/kidscount/indicator_briefs/teen_death.pdf

Silverman, P. R., Nickman, S., & Worden, W. J. (1992). Detachment revisited: The child's reconstruction of a dead parent. *American Journal of Orthopsychiatry, 62,* 494–503.

Silverman, P. R., & Worden, J. (1992). Children's reactions in the early months after the death of a parent. *American Journal of Orthopsychiatry, 62,* 93–104.

Spencer, M. B., Dupree, D., Cunningham, M., Harpalani, V., & Muñoz-Miller, M. (2003). Vulnerability to violence: A contextually-sensitive, developmental perspective on African-American adolescents. *Journal of Social Issues, 59,* 33–49.

Spungen, D. (1998). *Homicide: The hidden victims: A guide for professionals.* Thousand Oaks, CA: Sage Publications.

Stoppelbein, L., & Leilani, G. (2000). Posttraumatic stress symptoms in parentally bereaved children and adolescents. *Journal of the American Academy of Child and Adolescent Psychiatry, 39,* 1112–1119.

Temple, S. (1997). Treating inner-city families of homicide victims: A contextually oriented approach. *Family Process, 36,* 133–149.

Terr, L. C. (1991). Childhood traumas: An outline and overview. *American Journal of Psychiatry, 148,* 10–20.

Terr, L C., Bloch, D. A., Michel, B. A., Shi, H., Reinhardt, J. A., & Matayer, S. (1997). Children's thinking in the wake of Challenger. *American Journal of Psychiatry, 154,* 744–751.

Traisman, E. (1992). *Fire in my heart, ice in my veins.* Omaha, NE: Centering Corporation.

Tuckman, B. W. (1963). Developmental sequence in small group. *Psychological Bulletin, 63,* 384–399.

United States Department of Justice, Bureau of Justice Statistics (n.d.). Homicide trends in the U.S. Trends by race. Retrieved December 1, 2001, from http://www.ojp.usdoj.gov/bjs/homicide/race.htm

van der Kolk, B. A. (1998). The psychology and psychobiology of developmental trauma. In A. Stoudemire (Ed.) *Human behavior: An introduction for medical students* (pp. 383–399). New York: Lippincott-Raven.

Weick, A. (1992). Building a strengths perspective for social work. In D. Saleebey (Ed.), *The strength perspective in social work practice* (pp. 18–26). White Plains, NY: Longman Publishing Group.

Wilby, J. (1995). Transcultural counseling. Bereavement counseling with adolescents. In S. C. Smith & M. Pennells (Eds.), *Interventions with bereaved children* (pp. 232–240). London: Jessica Kingsley Publishing.

Worden, W. J. (1996). *Children and grief: When a parent dies.* New York: Guilford Press.

Worden, W. J., & Silverman, P. S. (1996). Parental death and the adjustment of school-aged children. *Omega, 33,* 91–102.

Yalom, I. D. (1995). *The theory and practice of group psychotherapy* (4th ed.). New York: Basic Books.

Index

Author Note

Alison Salloum, MSW, LCSW, is a licensed clinical social worker whose practice specializes in working with children and families affected by violence and loss. Ms. Salloum is working on her doctorate at Tulane University, School of Social Work. She is the senior clinical advisor for Project LAST, a program offered by the Children's Bureau, which provides therapeutic services for children and families exposed to violence.

Children's Bureau is a nonprofit agency that has been serving the needs of children and families in the Greater New Orleans area since 1892. Project LAST (Loss And Survival Team), an outreach program of the agency, works with children, adolescents, and their families who are survivors and/or witnesses of violence. For more information about Children's Bureau, visit their Web site at www.childrens-bureau.com.